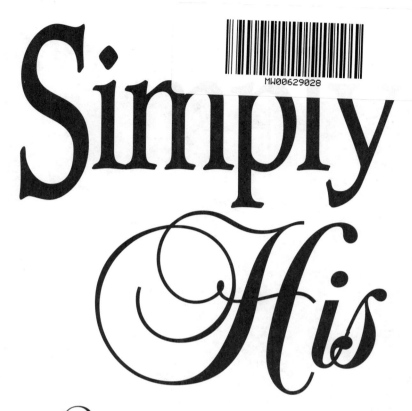

Simply His

A missionary story of love, commitment, and a willing heart

EUNICE PERRYMAN
PAM WADDELL

Woman's Missionary Union
Birmingham, Alabama

Woman's Missionary Union
P. O. Box 830010
Birmingham, AL 35283-0010

Dewey Decimal Classification: 266.009
Subject Headings: PERRYMAN, EUNICE HARRIS
                  MISSIONS, VOLUNTEER
                  MISSIONS—PERSONAL NARRATIVE

Unless otherwise noted, Scripture quotations are from the King James
Version of the Bible.

Cover design by Janell E. Young

ISBN: 1-56309-172-0
W964120•0496•5M1

This book is dedicated to the precious people who are such a real part of all that has happened to me.

A. L. and Myra Courtney and First Baptist Church, Pell City, Alabama

They commissioned me and set me apart for the work to which God had called me. My pastor, A. L. Courtney Jr., led my church family to walk with me every step of the way. They helped in the preparation for my journeys and held the ropes in prayer as I went. They supplied and maintained a home for me while I was away. When I came home on furlough, it was always ready, kept with so much tender, loving care that I always looked forward to spending my first night back in my own home. I thank God for First Baptist Church, Pell City.

Richard Lee and Betty Carmichael Harris

My brother, Richard, and his lovely wife, Betty, took on the total responsibility of all my financial affairs. Richard was given the power of attorney to handle the rental and subsequent sale of my farm. He and Betty kept my bank account reconciled monthly because my bank statements could not be sent overseas. Before I left for my first trip, I asked Richard if I should leave some extra money in my account. He told me he would take care of any problems and not to worry. What more could I ask? Greater love hath no man than this.

In addition to keeping my banking straight, paying bills, and filing tax returns, Betty wrote me every week. I could depend on a letter from home, full of news about everyone. When she learned I was taking the cards apart and keeping the fronts, she was always careful to just write on the other side. I used them for lessons.

Ida Florence Lee

My dearest friend and private prayer partner, Ida Florence, wrote every week. In most of her letters she included the church bulletin and kept me up-to-date with everyone in our church family. Many times she carried my prayer needs to the classes at church. She is very special.

Frances Morrison Perryman
Married to my youngest son, John, my dear daughter-in-law,
Frances, also wrote every week I was away. Her letters were
so prompt. The one week I did not get a letter from her, her father had taken ill and died. Frances will never know what receiving a letter each week meant to me. Her letters were
always full of news about my dear family.

To all of these dear friends, and to all who prayed me through
every experience, I say, *"Asanti sana"* (Swahili); *"Muchas
gracias"* (Spanish); *"Amasa ganalio"* (Amharic); *"Com sa
ham ne da"* (Korean); "Thanks, you guys" (North Dakotan).
　From the bottom of my heart, I pray this book shall be an
inspiration to all who read it. May God bless you!

　　　　　Simply His,

　　　　　Eunice Perryman

Contents

Introduction

Eunice Perryman is truly one of God's earthly angels. Anyone who knows her will agree that her compassion, love, and concern for others is truly Christ-centered. Prior to her call to missions, Eunice Perryman was one of our church's most active members. Her love for missions kept her at the center of every missions activity, emphasis, and study group. She was, and still is, a well-respected and endearing member of First Baptist Church, Pell City, Alabama.

Her subsequent call to the missions field came as no surprise to those who knew her. The church family embraced her decision with excitement and anticipation. At the time of her first missions trip we all felt a part of this glorious undertaking. Her unselfish desire to include her church family in all that took place drew her nearer to our hearts than ever before.

I taught Girls in Action (GA), the missions organization for girls in grades 1 through 6, and was very active in my Baptist Young Women (BYW) group. Every Wednesday night as the girls and I studied about missionaries around the world we also remembered Eunice Perryman. We especially remembered her on her birthday and holidays. Sometimes we recorded our own celebrations and sent them to her, and sometimes we gathered gifts and goodies and sent them to her. We always had great fun in decorating cards and letters to send. My BYW group celebrated her birthday, long-distance, by holding a party in her honor and recording our somewhat off-key rendition of "Happy Birthday!" Our prayers always ended with special requests for her. When she wrote to the church, she was good to include a special letter to our group. Her letters were full of funny stories, touching moments, and lots of prayer requests; always for others and seldom for herself. The reading of her letters was an integral part of our meetings.

I will always be grateful to Eunice Perryman for entrusting me with the task of helping her write this book. I was writing a small news column for a local newspaper and taking a course in writing in hopes of improving my proficiency. I will never forget the day she asked me to help. Sunday services had just concluded and people were enjoying the fellowship that follows a worship experience. She had been home on furlough only a short time and had shared some of her experiences with our church. She came up and asked if I would like to help her write her biography, like she was asking me if I'd like another piece of cake! She did not ask if I was qualified to help her. She did not ask if I had ever written a book before. She simply assumed I had the knowledge and experience to do the job. Her confidence in my ability really shook me up. All I could answer was, "Me?" I told her I would consider it an honor and I asked for time to pray about it. She smiled and told me to take all the time I needed.

I am amazed at how "God works all things together for good." I began to pray, asking for God's guidance. I had a full-time job, two young children, and spent a good deal of spare time interviewing people and writing for the local newspaper. I prayed that if God wanted me to help write this book, He would have to make the time for me to do it. My writing instructor told me it would be a tremendous undertaking for an inexperienced writer. I left it in God's hands.

I sometimes think God has a sense of humor when it comes to working out His timing. After a lot of prayer and soul searching, I felt such an excitement each time I thought about taking on this job. I knew God blessed my decision. Eunice Perryman and I began our plans. We knew we would need a lot of time at the beginning in order to get things moving, but did not know where we would find this time. God did. He gave me six weeks! It was no coincidence that I suddenly needed surgery that would require about six weeks to recuperate. I'll never know whether God caused the need, or whether He just had a hand in the timing, but I thanked Him for the help.

It has taken the two of us many years to complete this book, but we are convinced that God has been in control the entire time. I have grown spiritually during this time and have a much deeper appreciation for the unselfish, limitless love missionaries have for all of God's children. So many times we limit ourselves with insignificant worries and burdens. We lose sight of God's abundant grace and limitless power to overcome any disability we think we have. God sees only the good in all of us. His love and forgiveness is freely given. It is only our own self-doubt that keeps us from being used by Him Who made us. This story is one of love, commitment, and the willing heart of a very special woman. Her devotion to our Lord is equaled only by her willingness to be used. Yes, God can use a grandmother. He can use everyone willing to give their all to those they love. God can. He did.

Pam Waddell

1

Launch Out into the Deep

"Now when he had left speaking, he said unto Simon, 'Launch out into the deep, and let down your nets for a draught'"
(Luke 5:4).

No stars illuminated the sky that night. Except for an occasional bird chirping his night song, it was very peaceful and quiet. Yet, I felt strange and confused. The day had been like any other Sunday. My schedule had been the same—rising early to bake a chocolate pound cake for the singles I taught, then Sunday School and church until noon. After an afternoon visit to the nursing home, going to Training Union (now Discipleship Training), and evening worship, I went home.

Perhaps the day was unusual because the Sunday School lesson about Jesus leading Peter back out into the waters to cast his nets had spoken to me. That night as I lay in bed trying to sleep, the same phrase kept racing through my mind. *Launch out into the deep. Launch out into the deep.* Just as I drifted off to sleep I was awakened again by the same phrase, only this time it was louder. What was God trying to tell me?

I tried to reason it all out. It seemed I was doing all that I possibly could. Finally I prayed, *Lord, let's get all the facts out in the open. First, there is my age. I am nearing 60!* I was thoroughly convinced there was not much more that a person my age could do. I was serving as Woman's Missionary Union (WMU) director at First Baptist Church, Pell City, Alabama, and teaching a Sunday School class for singles. I also led a Bible study in a low-rent housing project, ministered to a nursing home in my community, and worked full time as a bookkeeper. Launch out into the deep . . . at my age?

Suddenly, a verse of Scripture flashed into my mind, illuminated as if by a flashlight. Abraham was called by God to go out into a land that God promised to show him. The light moved down, and it read, "And Abram was seventy and five years old when he departed out." I had known that Scripture passage all my life, but it had never really meant anything special. Showing me one example of age not being a problem was not enough. God also brought to my memory that Moses was 40 years old when he killed a man in Egypt. He was sent into the wilderness where he wandered for 40 more years. At the age of 80, God spoke to him from a burning bush and instructed him to lead His people out of bondage. If God used people so much older than me, surely He could use me. He had made His point perfectly clear.

The next hurdle to overcome was that I was divorced. It made a tremendous impact on my life. I sincerely believe that divorce is a sin. I was missing the mark on what God had planned for me. However, God's grace and forgiveness are bigger than any sin we commit. God reminded me of the sins of David and Moses. He used those men, even though they too had experienced sin in their lives. Why had I not realized that before? God is so great! He is not limited by my expectations.

God had been so patient with me—calling me to missions as a teenager and allowing me to choose another direction for my life instead. My decision to marry would change the entire course of my life. Shortly after marrying, I realized I had made a terrible mistake. Divorce was out of the question, so I made the best of it. There had never been a divorce in my family, and I knew my family would not approve. We had always been taught if you make your bed hard, you must lie in it.

I determined to settle down and try to be happy. Two precious sons and 39 years later, I realized that divorce was not an unpardonable sin. It was while attempting to read my Bible through in 1 year that God showed me one passage after another where sins were forgiven and people were able to be used by Him. I was to find out much later that God had a plan for me. After much prayer, I filed for divorce.

My decision to divorce was affirmed by God in so many ways. Miracles became almost a daily experience. His presence was so very real to me during that time. Each day came with the assurance from God that this was the right way to go. Now, after 40 years, God had once again called me to missions. This time I said yes!

At the close of this very special experience on that peaceful Sunday night, I saw myself walking up a mountain beside an older man and a young boy. The boy had a bundle of sticks on his back. I never saw their faces or heard a word they said. We came to a clearing, and the old man built an altar. When he finished, I placed myself on that altar. My prayer was, *Lord, if You can do anything more with me than You are already doing, then here I am. Use me anywhere You want to, Lord. Use me.* This can be a very dangerous statement if a person does not mean it. God took me at my word and began opening doors immediately.

2

The Impossible Dream of Serving

"Now therefore give me this mountain" (Josh. 14:12).

As we stood listening to the invitation the following Sunday, my heart was filled with peace at having answered God's call. I had not the remotest idea what God was calling me to do. I knew only that I must respond to whatever He had for me. I stepped out into the aisle and went to my pastor, A. L. Courtney Jr., and shared with him my experience the previous Sunday night. Together we prayed for God's guidance. I felt that even though I was already involved in missions organizations at church, God had something more for me to do. Later that week I talked with my pastor and his wife, Myra, at length about my decision. They were very supportive. Myra suggested I complete and send in a copy of a missions volunteer form we had at our church.

I received a prompt answer from the Mission Service Corps personnel at the Home Mission Board (HMB) and, excitedly, began filling out the application. It contained several pages of in-depth, personal questions concerning my spiritual gifts, abilities, beliefs, life history, and the type of work I wanted to do. I returned the application after much prayer and waited, anxiously, to hear from them.

Soon afterward, a letter arrived from the HMB requesting that I make reservations to attend an orientation in Atlanta, Georgia. Before going to Atlanta, I attended the Woman's Missionary Union (WMU) state convention which was being held in Huntsville, Alabama. One of the speakers at the meeting was Charles Bryan, vice-president of the Foreign Mission Board (FMB). I was introduced to him, and I asked if I could talk with him for a few minutes. There were so many questions I wanted to ask about serving on the missions field. He asked where I would be having lunch that day, and I told him I would be eating at the church. We decided to try to get together during lunch. Later that morning, while standing in the lunch line, I began to search for a place to sit. I saw him motioning for me to come sit beside him. There happened to be just one vacant seat. As we ate, I told him about myself and what it was I wanted to do. A letter had come from the FMB the previous week stating that they would consider me for service, even though I was divorced. I was very excited at this prospect, and I asked him what I should do. Bryan's advice was that I attend the orientation at the HMB because it would be beneficial to me regardless of where I served. He also advised me to call the FMB and get more information on what steps needed to be taken. My visit with him was very informative and helpful. I was thankful for the opportunity to talk with someone so knowledgeable.

I called the FMB the following week and talked with Frances Gordon. After speaking with her, I realized how fortunate I had been to talk with Charles Bryan personally. She told me that normally it took months to get an appointment with him. Charles Bryan later sent a letter to the Volunteers in Missions Department on my behalf. God had opened doors and provided all that I needed.

The FMB had several requirements for me, one being an interview with a psychologist. I enjoyed my talk with him, and when we were finished, he said, "Go home and get ready to fly."

I laughed and said, "I have been in orbit for the last three months!"

The FMB also examined the attitude of my church and my community toward me. Questions were asked about my divorce, children, and other personal information. God moved me through each step, opening doors and clearing my path of all obstacles. He knew just what had to be done!

I learned that as a volunteer I would have to pay my own expenses, including transportation to and from the field and special overseas insurance. My plans had been to wait until I was 62. At that time I would be eligible for Social Security retirement checks to help pay my expenses. My father died in December 1980, leaving me a small inheritance. My brother, Richard Lee Harris, and youngest son, John Jr., suggested that I use this money to finance my trips, allowing me to begin my service before the age of 62. I also had a farm which would need care. I had been praying for God to handle the selling or renting of my farm, but He had not seen fit to sell it, leaving me to feel that I could not leave until all the loose ends were settled. My brother offered to take care of selling or renting the farm. My sons were both working out of town and could not have assumed this responsibility. I did not want to impose on Richard and discussed this with my pastor. My pastor asked me if I wanted to see my family get involved with missions. He told me there was a fine line between imposing on them and getting them involved. I called my brother and accepted his offer. I gave him the power of attorney to care for all my personal business needs. God has continued to amaze me at how He puts everything in order.

While preparing to leave for my first assignment, I had many difficult decisions to make. One very difficult decision was the decision to sell most of my belongings. I would not need them and the money would certainly help. It was difficult for me to part with possessions I had accumulated over the last 60 years — special things such as china serving pieces given to me by cherished friends and family, linens which were hand-embroidered, and furniture which my children had enjoyed since their childhood. If it had not been for my friends helping me through that trying time it would have been much harder to part with these very personal possessions. My friends supported me and reassured me that this was the right thing to do.

As my time of departure drew near, I was blessed with friends and employers who wanted to get involved. My employer, John Fisher of Prairie Tank Southern, held a banquet in my honor and presented a bonus to me. The employees presented me with a 35mm camera, which I still use wherever God sends me. A previous employer, Mike Reinhardt, gave me a leather case for the camera and 24 rolls of slide film, including the money to have it developed. These gifts played a large part in my ministry, allowing me later to share these slides with different churches and organizations. Without them, my testimony would not have been as effective. Many friends and relatives helped to supply my every need.

A very precious memory of the many kindnesses shown me was a party given by several Sunday School classes at my church. They had prepared a lovely little tree and decorated it with money. There were three items I needed to purchase before I left: a large piece of luggage, a travel iron, and a travel alarm clock. The day after the party, I set out to purchase these items. After they were selected and paid for, the gifts from the money tree had paid for all three items, with 60 cents left over! Yes, every step of the way Ephesians 3:20–21 rang true. God had provided "exceeding abundantly above" my every need.

A special service was held by my church, First Baptist Church of Pell City, to commission me for this unusual undertaking. It was a very loving gesture in which my church family promised to pray for me daily. I would feel those prayers many times in the years to come. Clyde Dotson, who had served more than 40 years in southern Africa, spoke that night. He challenged me in ways I shall never forget. The efforts of Dotson and my pastor made my commissioning service a very special memory. Dave Milligan led in the dedicatory prayer. A reception followed the service.

Their expressions of concern for my welfare touched me greatly and made me more aware than ever before of God's wonderful grace. As the time for leaving neared, my son, John, came by for breakfast one morning. As we were looking over the maps I pointed out Mount Kilimanjaro. He said, "Mother, I remember as a child hearing you pray, 'Lord, give me a mountain to climb.'" Laughing, I told him that wasn't the kind of mountain I meant! He also remembered sermons ad-

8

monishing, "Be careful what you pray for." That conversation is a very special memory.

Only 14 months had passed since I answered God's call. He had given me another chance. God is so good to those who love Him. Two short days after my commissioning service, I stood waving good-bye to my family, pastor, and friends. Friday, September 25, 1981, I was on my way to Tanzania, Africa, praising God all the way. I could have flown without the plane. In fact, sleep came easily during my flight. When I arrived in Tanzania, I was anxious to get to work. We volunteers pride ourselves in being able to hit the ground running.

show them a simpler way of doing it. Martha had made the comment that they felt very inadequate. I could not imagine a nurse being inadequate at anything. I was delighted to go and was booked on the first plane going their way.

The Mission owned a Cessna 210 that was used to transport the missionaries from one part of the country to the other. Marty Akin coordinated these flights while her husband, Cordell, piloted the flights and made the arrangements. My trip was fantastic. I was able to see many parts of the country I might not have seen had it not been for my thoughtful pilot and guide. The countryside was beautiful. I was still amazed at the natural beauty Africa possessed.

It was a very special week for me. Janet's birthday, March 10, fell during that week. Martha and Janet had decided it would be better if Janet learned the bookkeeping and later taught it to Martha. When Martha walked in carrying a beautiful chocolate birthday cake, Janet was surprised to read the inscription which said, "Happy Birthday, Bookkeeper!" After learning for only two days, Janet was ready to take one month of records and record them into the books completely on her own. She knew that Southern Baptists everywhere were praying for her that day. The next morning at breakfast she remarked that people in the US were still praying for her because Tanzania was eight hours ahead of US time.

On Thursday, Cordell picked me up on his way to another stop. We took the scenic route all the way. We flew to the western area of Tanzania to Bukoba, where we stopped to pick up Betty Ann Whitson. Our next stop was in Kasulu, where we spent the night with agricultural missionaries Eva and Rollie Ennis. It was delightful to see them at work. Even though Rollie was not an ordained minister, he had started several churches in the area where they lived. God's grace is always sufficient.

I will never forget the morning we left. Eva gave me some spices to make pork sausage. This does not sound very special, but in Africa pork sausage is not available. While Eva and Rollie were home on furlough, they had contacted a local sausage company and asked for their recipe, explaining that they were foreign missionaries in Tanzania. They could kill warthogs to make the sausage, but they needed to know what spices to put in it. Instead of giving them the recipe, the sausage company sent them a large box of spices already mixed and ready to add to the meat. Eva and Rollie were sharing these with all the missionaries who came their way. I could buy the ground pork and make my own. It was a real treat to have good old US sausage!

On the return flight, we experienced a little trouble. The engine began to backfire. Cordell and Betty Ann Whitson, who were in the front seats, tried to keep me from realizing what was happening; but I was already aware that something was wrong. Knowing that our God was all-powerful and in control put me at ease. I just talked with Him and soon felt that wonderful, comforting peace. God was so very real and present. He was in complete control. Before we landed at Mwanza, Cordell radioed in and asked a Missionary Aviation Fellowship (MAF) pilot to meet us and take us into Arusha. As we prepared to land, Cordell hesitated. A Russian MiG was just taking off. The airport did not have ground control to guide the planes in and out, so we had to be very careful. Once on the ground, we waited a few hours for the other plane. I asked Cordell how he would know when to take off again. He said he had counted ten Russian MiGs being used to train the Tanzanian air force. When all ten were on the ground, we would leave. His idea worked. Regardless of the circumstances, God was in control.

The airport was at the edge of beautiful Lake Victoria. Cordell had scheduled my return so that I could see some of the western part of Tanzania. Instead of taking me directly north from Mbeya to Arusha, I was privileged to see three other Mission stations. I was very grateful to him for showing me the beautiful countryside. Cordell explained that it was his way of thanking the volunteers for their help. He liked to show them as much of the country as possible.

The MAF pilot took us home. We left Cordell at the airport trying to get customs and immigration to let him fly directly to Kenya to repair the plane. He finally got permission, obtained the necessary permits, and took off. Unfortunately, the trouble worsened and he was forced to turn back. The MAF sent a mechanic out to make repairs. The fuel pump was repaired and Cordell was on his way.

I was so glad when we finally arrived in Arusha. In one short week I had gone from north Tanzania, to the far eastern coast of Dar es Salaam, into central Tanzania, to southern Tanzania, into the western area, and back home. It once again reminded me that faith is going as far as you can see and one step more. When faithful prayer supporters at home promise to hold the ropes for missionaries, you never realize how much they really depend on you. I am so glad that God promised His grace would be sufficient for our every need.

It was urgent that I reach home on Friday because the Arusha Baptist Church was coming for a picnic in my backyard on Saturday. All went well and preparations were made for the picnic. Everyone had a delightful time of fun, food, and fellowship.

4

The Gift—A Contented Heart

"For I have learned, in whatsoever state I am, therewith to be content" (Phil. 4:11b).

It had never occurred to me that only Americans celebrated Thanksgiving. My first Thanksgiving in Tanzania was very special. All the Americans in Tanzania came together at Lake Duludi and had a delightful evening. It was a covered-dish supper, and I fixed a large roast and a banana pudding. I could not think of anything more American. There were 99 of us there. During the evening someone asked, "Does anyone know Eunice Perryman?" He had a friend whom I had met at orientation, and she had asked him to look me up. He was with the Peace Corps. I soon adopted Robert Harrison.

Hunting season in Tanzania was from July 1 through December 31. When Charles and Betty Bedenbaugh planned a day of hunting, they insisted I go along. The hunting and killing of animals is something I have never enjoyed, but after much encouragement I agreed to go. We left about 4:00 A.M. with our lunches and cold drinks packed, and headed toward an area where hunting was allowed.

Charles had a good day of hunting, killing several wildebeests, grants, impalas, and others. The all-terrain vehicle was loaded with meat which they had cut up. It is the custom there to cut out the good parts, such as the quarters, back loin, etc., and leave the rest for the carnivorous animals to clean up. By the end of the day, the vehicle was full. The odor was terrible, and blood was running off the top of the roof and down the windows. This particular vehicle was used mainly for hunting, so it was not as bad as it sounds.

We were on our way out of the hunting area when a large truck overtook us. Six men jumped out of the truck waving machine guns at us and ordered us to get out of the vehicle. Everyone quickly jumped out, except me. My door was stuck! Immediately one of the men came over to me and ordered me again, in Swahili, to get out. He saw that I could not open my door and reached over to help me get it open. Seeing that I was elderly, he even helped me out. Boy, was I glad that Tanzanians have a great respect for the elderly. I thanked God for my 61 years!

We were ordered to sit down. Sitting on that dusty road, we must have looked like a flock of birds perched on a wire! They kept their guns on us while they examined Charles's license. They kept talking to him in Swahili, making it hard for me to understand what they wanted. I was sure they wanted either some of the meat, or some other bribe. After about three hours of harassment we were allowed to leave. During the hunt we had seen a large hardbacked turtle. Thinking the children in Arusha would enjoy it, we had loaded it into the vehicle. The men fussed because we did not have a license for turtle. When they allowed us to leave, one of the soldiers picked up the turtle and handed it to me! They were all very scornful of us, but this particular man had a soft spot for me. I did not want to touch the turtle, but could not refuse taking it from him. After three long hours these men understood that people with the Baptist Mission do not submit to bribes very easily. Once again God was with us, His ever-present protection so evident!

The day after the hunt Charles brought me a hindquarter of a grant. He laid it across my kitchen cabinet. I asked what I was to do with it. He explained that this was my meat for the next six months. I told him I had never butchered meat, so he sharpened my knives and showed me how to cut it down through the seams. He explained how to cool it; slice it into steaks, roasts, and stew meat; and grind the leftovers into hamburger meat. He explained that since I had no freezer bags I would need to go to the hardware store and get polyethylene tubing to make the freezer bags.

I was delighted to see my friend from the Peace Corps, Robert Harrison, at this particular time. He went to the hardware store and brought back two kilos of polyethylene. We lit a candle and sliced off eight-inch sections of tubing, sealing one end by running it over the burning candle. I chose to make the bags while Robert cut the meat. We filled them with meat and sealed the other end. Finally all the meat was ready for the freezer. How good God is. He really does supply every need.

Christmas was a very special time in Tanzania. There is not a lot of commercialism there, nor Christian celebration. I saw only one or two stores with tinsel ropes in their windows or Christmas greetings displayed. The International Little Theatre planned and produced a beautiful Christmas pageant which I enjoyed immensely. It was quite different from pageants in the US. For the first time in my life, I saw a Black baby Jesus, Joseph, and Mary. There were even Black angels! At the end of the pageant, as Mary and Joseph started to leave the stage, Mary tied the baby on her back African style.

Early in December, I began to feel a little dread as we started preparing for the Christmas season. I had never been away from my children and grandchildren at all, much less during Christmas. This was a new experience for me. I had the nagging feeling that sooner or later I would break down.

I am continually reminded of God's sufficient grace. Everyone in Tanzania tried so hard to see that I had everything I needed. When the missionaries made a trip to Kenya they would bring back anything I needed—and more! They even brought some Christmas candy for me to enjoy. Santa Claus had come early. No, every good and perfect gift is from above. I thank God for every one of them!

My pastor at the Baptist church in Arusha, Lee Ray Greene, and his precious wife, Beth, along with Robert Harrison, came home with me after church many times. Their favorite meal was chicken and dumplings. They raved about the meals, declaring to write their families in the States about my dumplings. When it was time to go, they all hugged my neck, just as my own family would have. God knew I needed young people. They could never take the place of my own family, but they shared their love with me and I with them. I thanked the Lord for bringing me to Tanzania.

On December 22, 1981, I was invited to have supper with Charles and Betty Bedenbaugh and their family. Some friends from Germany and Australia were there. We all enjoyed their beautiful Christmas tree. I cherish the lovely orchid necklace given me that night by Charles and Betty.

On December 23 we all went to a joint service of all the area churches. The highlight of the service was when "Silent Night" was sung. Five different families, dressed in native clothing, sang that song in their native languages. The choir sang the first verse in English, then from different areas of the church, each family sang a verse in their own language. "Silent Night" was sung in French, Italian, German, and Swahili. The last verse was sung by the entire audience, each person singing in his or her own language. Only God could have brought the joy we felt that night. It was wonderful.

Bill and Janice Oliver invited me to their home for Christmas Eve. It was a very special night for me. Their three children needed a grandmother and I enjoyed being one. They even had gifts for me. I had nothing in return but a fresh coconut cake. The children seemed to enjoy giving the gifts instead of receiving them. I returned home that night, happy, content, and looking forward to the surprise I had for all my "family" in Arusha.

About two months earlier, while visiting with an area butcher, I had asked what I would have to do to get a cured ham. His answer was that people in a socialist country do not have cured ham. He was a delightful man who had escaped from Poland and come to Tanzania, opening a butcher shop in his garage. I was not to be stopped and asked again if I could get a cured ham.

He answered, "There is no salt."

I offered to supply the salt, being fortunate enough to have some. He said he would see what he could do. Early in December during one of my visits to his shop, the Polish butcher left the garage and went out to a small outbuilding.

His wife said, "I think he has something special for you." When he returned, he sliced a small piece off the ham he was carrying and handed it to me. Unless you have done without cured ham for months, you cannot imagine how delicious it tasted! It was the size of a picnic ham, approximately 7 kilos, or 15 pounds. The cost was 720 shillings and at the currency ratio of eight to one, this was $90 in US currency! Since all the missionary families in Arusha were to eat Christmas dinner with me, I was willing to splurge. It was worth every penny when that baked ham was brought to our Christmas table and I saw the delight on their faces!

I just knew there would come a time when I would long for my family at home. This was the first Christmas I had ever spent apart from my loved ones. There were so many people who expressed their love for me, and I for them, that I felt no loss during this special time. After examining all the possibilities, I decided I was where I wanted to be. Without a doubt I was where God wanted me to be. He had indeed supplied my every need.

One of the guests at my home during Christmas was my special friend from the Peace Corps, Robert Harrison. He had promised to come in from the bush where he was stationed in time to have Christmas dinner with us. Robert had not arrived by 11:00 A.M. and I was beginning to worry. He lived four hours away and would be coming on his motorcycle. About 1:00 P.M. just as we were about to eat, he arrived. He had stopped along the way to help someone whose car had broken down. After Robert had a quick bath to wash off the dust, we were ready to share our Christmas dinner. God saw to it that I felt no loss during this special time of year.

I missed my children and grandchildren very much, so I adopted all the young people in the area where I served. I especially enjoyed Robert Harrison. He came in from the bush about every two weeks. Being only 28 years old, he was always hungry! The only foods in the bush were bananas and eggs. He could not carry a lot of groceries on his motorcycle, so I expected him every two weeks. He would finish off all my leftovers. Robert always needed to talk. Most of the time he never saw a white face until he got to Arusha. Every time he asked the blessing, it always concluded with, "Thank You, Father, for having Eunice here." Robert insisted I keep a list of things that needed repairing, and when he visited, he would repair them for me. I also thanked the Lord for him!

One memory I have of my time in Arusha was an unexpected visit with Harold Mitchell, one of our missionaries in Tanzania. A telephone call came in one day from Harold. He was stranded at the Kilimanjaro Airport in Moshi. All of the missionaries living in Moshi were away from home. He had called all he knew in Arusha and also found that none were at home. As a last resort he had called me. The airport was about an hour's drive from Arusha, and it was already getting dark. He specifically said for me not to come alone. I did not argue, but knew that God would accompany me. As I was leaving I saw my handyman, Sinai, working in the garden. I called to him and asked if he would like to ride to the airport with me. He was delighted and ran to change clothes.

When we arrived at the airport, we learned that Harold had accompanied another of our missionaries to Nairobi, Kenya, earlier that day. Larry Thomas was very sick. Harold had sat with him all night and then had taken him to Nairobi the next day. Harold took a flight back as far as Moshi, thinking he could get another flight to Dar es Salaam before night. When he saw me, he hugged me and said, "I thank God that He had you here in Tanzania." God found such wonderful ways to affirm my belief that I was right where he wanted me!

When we got back to Arusha, I offered to take him to any of the other homes to spend the night. I knew the policy of not having a man stay in a home where there was only one woman present.

Harold said, "Eunice, I have not slept in 36 hours. Can I just please stay here?"

Of course, I agreed; and while he was getting cleaned up, I prepared hot biscuits, impala steaks, and gravy. I had made a coconut pie and potato salad that afternoon, just in case someone dropped by. He had a good meal and went right to bed. I was thankful that God had brought me to Tanzania. Thereafter, Harold called me his guardian angel. Larry Thomas was diagnosed with a malignancy and died three weeks later in Nairobi, Kenya.

One of the most precious couples in Tanzania was journeyman Lee Ray Greene and his wife, Beth. They were there to pastor our Baptist church in Arusha. They lived at the seminary about ten miles from Arusha. The Arusha Baptist Church not only held English Sunday School classes but also Swahili classes. Many times I filled in teaching the adult class and loved every minute of it. We did not have literature for our classes, so if missionaries were visiting, they would sometimes teach our group. Other times they just wanted to listen.

One morning after teaching a lesson in which all had participated, I was shocked to learn that five in the class held doctorates. God had used me, with no college and no seminary training, to lead the discussion. It seemed my lack of credentials never stopped God from taking the loaves and fishes and multiplying them to make them sufficient.

Lee Ray and Beth always included me in picnics, trips to game parks, drives into the bush, or just visiting in the homes of nationals. They were precious and just another example of God letting me adopt young people. Most of all Lee Ray liked my chicken and dumplings. In fact, if he ever learned of anyone who had chickens for sale, he would buy them and bring them to me. Good chickens were hard to find and very expensive. One could take a single chicken and flavor a large pot of dumplings to feed 20 people. One of the first things I wanted to do after arriving back in the US was to fill up on fried chicken!

5

God's Delights and Surprises

"But as it is written, Eye hath not seen, nor ear heard, neither have entered into the heart of man, the things which God hath prepared for them that love him" (1 Cor. 2:9).

Although there was not a lot of entertainment such as we are accustomed to in the US, we still enjoyed our evenings and weekends. There was no television and all radio broadcasts were in Swahili, except the shortwave stations. The only broadcasts of interest to us were the news reports. As an alternative to quiet nights, we enjoyed sharing a meal together and playing table games, but most of all we enjoyed the fellowship we shared with one another. Many times our group was joined by other missionaries stopping over for the night. This was always a blessing.

The highlight of any missionary's life was to receive packages from the US. I was no different. Once I received a box of goodies from my brother, Richard, and his wife, Betty. I was excited to find items such as yeast, cake mix, gelatin dessert, tissues, cheeses, etc. This particular box also contained two eight-ounce pieces of solid milk chocolate. They had traveled so far, taking about six months to arrive, and they had not broken. This was the third box of goodies Richard and Betty had sent.

As God would have it, that very night Jim and Molly Houser and pilot, Cordell Akin, arrived to spend the night. We shared that wonderful chocolate and the love that went with it.

Another dear friend, Pete Little, also sent me a box of goodies while I was in Africa. This particular box contained,
among other things, a large jar of peanut butter. It must have
contained 30 ounces. It lasted my entire stay in Africa, allowing many special people to enjoy it. One night while several
missionaries were there for the night, I asked, "If you could
have any kind of candy you wanted, what would you want?"

Cordell Akin replied, "peanut butter cups."

I went to the refrigerator and brought out a bag of peanut
butter cups!

Cordell's eyes lit up as he exclaimed, "I can't believe it!"

So many friends at home kept me supplied with goodies so
faithfully, and I loved sharing them. It made my friends at home
even more special. Every day is special when you are where
God wants you to be; and doing what God wants you to do.

On March 25, 1982, I received a special telex. It read, "Hi,
Grandmother. My name is Michael Frank Perryman. I arrived
at 8:57 P.M. on March 23. I weigh 7 pounds, 7 ounces. I am
great, and my mom is great, too; so is Dad and Brother and
Sister."

This was a wonderful surprise. When I left home in September, all four grandchildren were almost grown. Frank and
Sue's other two children, Kenneth Dean, 21, and Donna
Renee, 18, were young adults. It was a real surprise to learn
there would be a new addition to their family. John and
Frances's children, John Carlton III, 24, and Lexie Sue, 20,
were also grown when I left home. In fact, my grandchildren
told me at the airport as I was leaving, that there was something wrong with the picture. They were supposed to be the
risk takers, and I should be staying home. Our newest addition
was a thrill to all of us.

I am firmly convinced that God is the biggest risk taker I
know. He had a full-time job just taking care of me. Around
every corner I could have fallen flat on my face, but God was
so very sufficient.

One morning I awakened to find I had lost my glasses. I

knew I had worn them to Bible study the night before. I remembered seeing the chain on them in the car. I thought I might have dropped them on the seat. I went into the kitchen and saw out the window that the dog was swinging something in his mouth, something that looked like my glasses. He had jumped on me the night before and had evidently pulled them off. He was a huge dog and one of my biggest problems. I went outside and successfully got the glasses away from him. He had chewed the ear pieces and left teeth marks on the frame, but my glasses were all right. Thank You, Lord! The dog had played with them all night, but God had taken care of them.

Another Sunday morning as I stepped outside to feed the dog before leaving for Sunday School, the door closed behind me and locked. Just inside the door were my Bible, Sunday School books, purse, and keys to the house and car. The handyman and I tried everything without success. I finally decided to walk the three blocks to Ed and Nancy Giddens's home. If they could not help me get into the house, at least I could ride to church with them. After going over every possibility, the Giddenses' young son, Josh, said he could get into the house through a window. It seemed impossible, but with God all things are possible. We went back to the house and Josh crawled through a window, ran to the door, and let us in. I knew that God once used a little boy's lunch to feed the multitudes, but on this day He used a precious little missionaries' kid (MK) I learned to love dearly.

God was taking care of me full-time. Many such instances were to take place over the next 10 years, and I never ceased to be amazed at how gracious God is. His patience with me was everlasting. Every instance reminded me of the many friends and family who were praying for me at home. God answered every prayer.

Many times when the mail came, I received 10 to 20 letters. Sometimes I shared my letters with missionaries who did not receive any mail. We passed around many of my letters from precious friends and family.

Sometimes I would use carbon to make six or eight copies at a time since we didn't have a copy machine. There were so many thoughts and experiences I wanted to share with so many people. I always added a page of personal correspondence with each letter. At the beginning of my assignment, I closed many of my letters with *Finally—In His Service.* As time went on my favorite closing became *Simply His.* I heard from many who read my letters whom I did not know prior to my leaving. I was to learn that several family members and friends made copies of my letters and shared them with co-workers and other friends. It was a delight to find that my brother, Richard, was doing this at his office. When I returned home, I had numerous friends from his office who knew all about me, yet I had never met them. I enjoyed writing letters home and sharing all the exciting things that were happening and all the wonderful things I was learning. Two very dear ones, Betty Harris, my sister-in-law, and Ida Florence Lee, a very dear friend, saved all their letters from me.

We had a wonderful revival at the Arusha Baptist Church. We really experienced the Holy Spirit moving in many hearts. I was so glad, for Jesus' sake, and also for Lee Ray Greene's sake. He and Beth had been so concerned because they had not seen much response in the church. During these revival services, there were 19 to profess faith in Christ as Savior. In the closing session we all stood and sang "When the Roll Is Called Up Yonder," each in our own native language. There was not a dry eye in the church. I am sure that must be what heaven will be like. It was indescribable. God is so great!

It was always a delight to work with missionaries who had a sense of humor. Everywhere I went there was much teasing, but everyone knew that all the teasing was done in love. I cherished it all.

Once, while a group was gathered at my house, Charles Bedenbaugh said, "I have never been stopped and searched while hunting, but take Eunice along and watch what happens! We never had trouble with the airplane, but take Eunice along and see what happens!" He finally concluded, "If you want to be where the action is, just take Eunice!" I treasure those moments of teasing.

I was once asked what my pastor thought about my trip. I answered, "He probably wonders when I am going to settle down and just be a normal missionary."

From the letters I received, people did not believe all of this could happen to normal, ordinary people. My experiences destroyed the myth that God only calls extraordinary people.

Once, during a conversation with Harold Mitchell, he said, "Eunice, there are so many people in the United States who feel that divorce or reaching the age of 60 is the end of the world. You should write a book entitled, *The Beginning—Not the End*." I promised him that if I ever found the time I would.

About six months into my first year, the personnel director of the Baptist Mission of Tanzania, Betty Ann Whitson, one of the most committed missionaries I've ever met, approached me regarding further work in Tanzania. She asked if I would consider coming back to Tanzania and working at the seminary while the business manager, Cecil Williams, and his wife, Aline, went home on furlough. There would be five months between the Williamses' departure, and the Swanns' arrival. I asked for time to pray about it.

When I talked with her again, I explained that I could not afford to return to the States and then come back because I paid for all my expenses out of my own pocket. I told her that if she had another job I could do until then, I would consider staying on.

I am convinced that nothing happens by coincidence. I believe God was in control, timing each detail so that everything worked perfectly. The five months between the two furloughs was the same span of time a volunteer hostess/caterer was needed for the Huruma Conference Center in Iringa, Tanzania.

When I talked with Betty Ann about this, I explained that although I was not experienced in catering, I did love to cook for large groups. I also told her I could not prepare African dishes. Her answer was, "We do not want you to cook African dishes. We have nationals for that. We want you to cook Alabama dishes." That's all I needed to hear.

At the completion of my first assignment, the Mission transported me to the conference center in Iringa. Much to my delight, I was to work with two Alabama missionaries, Larry and Sandra Scales, and their daughter, Rebecca.

6

The Gift of Serving

"But the fruit of the Spirit is love, joy, peace, longsuffering, gentleness, goodness, faith, meekness, temperance: against such there is no law" (Gal. 5:22–23).

The Huruma Conference Center where I was to serve for the next five months is a beautiful example of what volunteers can do when committed to follow God's leading. The manager of the center, Larry Scales, was one of the first volunteers from North Augusta Baptist Church in South Carolina to come and help build the conference center. At that time Larry was serving as associate pastor; but upon his arrival back in the States, he and his wife, Sandra, contacted the Foreign Mission Board (FMB) to sign up for foreign mission service.

The audit of the treasurer's office in Arusha had been postponed several times. After I moved to Iringa, the audit was finally completed. Charles Bedenbaugh wrote me to say that it had received an A1 rating. I really needed to hear such good news, for this had been my first assignment with the FMB. God had affirmed that this was where He wanted me to be. Now at the conference center, I was with more nationals and had a very different assignment.

After I made the decision to go to Iringa, it occurred to me that my clothing was not sufficient. Iringa is located in the mountains, with temperatures falling into the 30s during the winter. Since I would be there from May until October, Tanzania's winter, my summer clothing would not do. The temperature had remained between 65°F and 90°F year-round in Arusha.

I needed only to voice my thoughts. Those precious missionaries shared their clothing with me and every need was met, right down to my long handles. During one especially cold period, while two summer missionaries were staying in Iringa, the three of us began walking from one place to another, side by side, with me in the middle, using our body heat to keep warm! Of course, I was feeding them well, so they wanted to see that I stayed healthy.

Larry Scales's first greeting to me when I arrived was, "I don't care if you never touch the kitchen, if you will only straighten out the books." Needless to say, I adopted Larry and his family as my own.

The men at the Mission and some of the volunteers had combined two bedroom units at the center, making a small two-room flat. All the units contained two bunk beds and a bathroom. When my little apartment was completed, I had the only one-bedroom flat in Tanzania with two bathrooms. I learned recently that they have since made one of those bathrooms into a laundry room. The ingenuity of missionaries never ceases to amaze me.

My first job at the center was to set up bookkeeping. I thoroughly enjoyed it. Most people hate to do bookkeeping, so there was much appreciation expressed. Larry was delighted with my work. My five months at the conference center were very busy. Sandra took me to the markets, bakery, etc. She taught me how to find vegetables, fruits, eggs, and staples. It was a delight to learn a new way to plan meals. We did the shopping first and then planned the meals with whatever we bought. It was a real learning experience. Once I became oriented, it fell my lot to make the desserts, a task I had always enjoyed. Making pie crusts had always been one of my weak spots, but making as many as 12 in one day brought new meaning to practice makes perfect.

I am sure that the missionaries did not enjoy eating my food anymore than I enjoyed preparing it. It did not take long to learn that coconut and chocolate pies, banana pudding, eclairs, and lemon custards were their favorites. Some people may have called it a job, but I called it heaven. All my life I had prayed for missionaries, studied about missionaries, and taught about missionaries. To be placed in their midst to do something for them was exceeding abundantly above all I could ever have asked or even thought.

On September 10, 1982, I celebrated my 62d birthday. I had been cooking for 25 people while attending a three-week refresher course in Swahili. At the start of the third week, I went into the dining hall for breakfast and was greeted with the a loud chorus of "Happy Birthday!" The missionaries gave me a long list of errands to run, which kept me in town until lunchtime. When I returned, I entered the dining hall to find a wonderful lunch waiting, complete with coconut cake and another round of "Happy Birthday!"

The children had made gifts, raided flower beds, made birthday cards, and hung balloons on my door. Some of the women had knitted houseshoes and made two beautiful banana baskets with gorgeous pictures of animals on them. Some had brought their own candy, chewing gum, gelatin dessert, etc.

The celebration lasted all day. It was wonderful. Even though I was 15,000 miles from home, there was joy in my heart. Someone once said, "Joy is the flag on the pole of the castle of the heart when the King is within." And truly, when Jesus is in the heart, regardless of location or circumstances, there is joy. I later received pictures taken back home of the birthday party my Sunday School class held in my honor. Yes, God is so good to give me such a family!

During my time in Iringa, I missed attending an English-speaking church. On Wednesday nights Larry and Sandra held an English-speaking Bible study at their home. We had a good group whose members represented many faiths. On Sunday all the church services were in Swahili. One day I asked Larry and Sandra if their daughter, Rebecca, could come to my flat for Sunday School. She was delighted because Swahili churches did not have age-level classes. So each Sunday we had a lesson on the flannel-graph, and Rebecca learned the books of the Bible. She was an excellent student and I enjoyed having her.

7

My First Real Missions Trip

"If ye abide in me, and my words abide in you, ye shall ask what ye will, and it shall be done unto you" (John 15:7).

One day I received a call from Janet McDowell, a nurse whom I helped learn a simpler way of bookkeeping. She wanted me to come to Mbeya to spend a week with her. She had already discussed this with Larry and Sandra. All the arrangements were made and I began to make my plans. Martha McAllister, another nurse, was on furlough, and Janet was anxious for me to come. This was something we had talked about often and it was finally going to come about.

My first weekend in Mbeya began by attending a Sunday worship service and baptism out in the bush. Franklin Fowler, medical director from the FMB and his wife, Dorcas, joined Keith and Peggy Oliphint, missionaries in the Mbeya association, Janet McDowell, and me for the service. It was held in a small church with a thatched roof. Afterward we walked for almost an hour to an irrigation ditch where the baptism was held. No one had warned me to leave my hose and heels at home, so I learned the hard way. It was high noon and we were just below the equator. The sun was beaming. That morning some of the men had gone ahead to dig out the ditch and build a temporary dam so the water would be deep enough for the baptism. However, a woman who had come to do her laundry had broken the dam, so the water was only about six inches deep. When the pastor dipped the candidates into the water it did not cover them, so he just rolled them over and over until they were sufficiently wet. These people were so serious about their baptism; the lack of water seemed of little concern. My, how much we take for granted in America.

I am so grateful that Davis Saunders, area director of Eastern and Southern Africa at that time, insisted I write a report of my experiences before the excitement faded. That report documented the greatest week of my life.

I had no idea what a bookkeeper would be able to do on a clinic trip, especially a bookkeeper not versed in the local languages, but God was in control. Janet said I could use the flannel-graph during the clinics. I had never spoken while someone translated, but Janet said, "Don't worry about language barriers. We will take care of that." While making my plans to go with Janet, I had written my pastor asking what I should teach. I wondered how to share with people who do not have bread about the Bread of life.

On September 28, 1982, loaded with supplies, and after lots of prayer, we set off for the bush. Janet; her assistant, Rhoda Kasengwa; Lucia Mwaipaja, a nurse and midwife who would weigh and register the mothers and children; Keith Oliphint; and I were ready to go. Just before we arrived at the clinic we stopped and took on one more passenger, Mzee Mathayo, pastor of Ilindi village. He had made all the necessary arrangements. He provided a lunch of *ugali* and chicken and his home for our overnight stay. He and his family moved into another hut for the night. They were lovely hosts.

We held the clinic in the Ilembo association. This association consists of 26 satellite churches, located so no one has to walk longer than two hours to attend church. It is also one of the oldest Baptist associations in Tanzania. We arrived around 10:00 A.M. The clinic was held in a two-room hut with a path to an outhouse, built especially for Anglo guests. There were about 50 mothers waiting for us when we arrived. The nurses treat expectant mothers and children up to age 5 .

After we unloaded the four-wheel drive vehicle and set up for the clinic, we assembled in the yard for a time of worship.

Keith Oliphint brought the message in Swahili. Surprise! This tribe did not speak Swahili. The chairman of the Ilembo association, Ebrahim Mtela, translated Keith's message from Swahili into Umalila. I began to wonder what on earth I would be able to do, considering I did not speak either language.

When the service ended, they held a teaching session on the basics of health care and gave instructions on how to run the clinic. About 12:30 P.M. the nurses called their first ten patients. I began the flannel-graph lessons. I taught, Keith Oliphint translated into Swahili, and Ebrahim Mtela translated into Umalila. After about 30 minutes, we took a break while the nurses called another group of patients. During this break Keith met with the crowd in small groups, witnessing with an interpreter and using tracts. The local pastors then followed his lead, witnessing to groups or one-on-one. When all the counseling halted, I started another session on flannel-graph. We held several of the sessions, with counseling continuing during each break. This first day was a holiday, so most of the village attended, including many men and even more children. As the day wore on, the crowd grew, but I could see no visible results.

We got an early start the second day. Just as I began my lesson, we noticed a large group of people coming toward us. Keith asked me to wait to begin until we could find out what was happening. The village chairman stood up and addressed the group, saying, "These people are kind enough to bring us medicine and help us. The least we can do is listen to what they have to say." He had brought the whole school to spend the entire day. He motioned for the children to sit close to the front. A group of about 50 boys came and sat on the right. We all applauded. Then came a group of girls who sat on the left. We also greeted them with applause.

I had not received an answer from my pastor before we left, and in my excitement, I had difficulty deciding what to teach. I finally decided on teaching Christ's life; including the angel appearing to Mary, the shepherds, manger, wise men, highlights of Christ's adult life, then the cross, empty tomb, and ending with the Living Lord. Because the whole school arrived, I ask Keith if I should teach, thinking maybe he should. He told me to continue.

I said, "Well, all I can do is depend on the Holy Spirit."

Keith grinned and said, "Ah, what a spot to be in!"

At that moment I realized that this was where the Lord was leading me all the time. I gave Keith a hug, and for the rest of the day, taught each session through my tears—partly out of the compassion I knew Jesus must have felt when he looked at the multitudes, and partly out of gratitude for God's graciousness to me. I am reminded of God's promise in Psalm 126:6, "He that goeth forth and weepeth, bearing precious seed, shall doubtless come again with rejoicing, bringing his sheaves with him." Yes, He is so great—and He does keep his promises.

I began each session with John 3:16, and God's love was the theme of them all. The Lord used everything I had ever learned from His Word. The Holy Spirit was very real.

We held sessions all day, breaking each hour for counseling in small groups. I was not aware at the time, but the Sunday night prior to my trip into the bush, my pastor had shared my letter with my home church, and a special prayer was offered for our ministry. My heart had been burdened since arriving in Tanzania that I had not won one soul to the Lord. I had asked them to specifically pray for at least one person to accept Christ.

At the end of the session, after talking about the Living Savior, I asked Keith to hold an invitation. He said I should do it. I had never given a public invitation in my life. Again, God was sufficient. We offered the invitation and there were 15 professions of faith. A lot of counseling followed until each pastor was convinced the decisions were real. Later that afternoon I noticed two young women coming toward the clinic holding hands. One of the women who attended the earlier session was bringing a friend. They found the local pastor, Mchungaji Sauti, sat down on the grass, and talked. He then took her over to Ebrahim, and he counseled with her. Later, we were shown the 16th name. What a day!

Keith later questioned the local pastor, concerned that some of the young people may have made decisions because a friend had. He explained that it was very unlikely, saying if they allowed their name to be put on a list, they were very serious. Pastor Sauti planned to work with the young people two days a week to continue their growth in Christ.

I must confess that my faith was as small as a mustard seed. My prayers were that God would call at least one soul, but in His marvelous grace, we received much fruit for our labors. May we never lose the excitement of seeing souls come to Christ. During all this time, the nurses saw more than 300 patients in two days. I never knew there was so much love and so much happiness to be found in Africa. In spite of any problems the happiest place in the world is right where God wants you to be. My favorite verse describes my experiences. "Now unto him who is able to do exceeding abundantly above all that we ask or think, according to the power that worketh in us, unto him be glory in the church by Christ Jesus throughout all ages, world without end" (Eph. 3:20–21).

I was left in charge of the conference center my last two weeks there, while the Scaleses attended a conference in Brackenhurst. On several nights, guests came by, needing a place to spend the night. It seemed too soon for me to be returning to Arusha. The Scaleses returned and soon we heard the familiar buzz of the plane passing overhead, telling me it was time to go. It was a very different lifestyle from America, but living it was a wonderful learning experience. There is still victory in Jesus, and hallelujah, He is letting you and me be a part of that victory!

8

Life at the Seminary

"In all these things we are more than conquerors through Him that loved us" (Rom. 8:37).

The International Baptist Theological Seminary has a lovely campus. It has many beautiful flowers which various missionaries have planted during their stay there. As planned earlier, it was to be my home on my return to Arusha. I was to stay in the business manager's home and use his vehicle.

It was a delight to find that I would be able to use the handyman who had worked for Cecil and Aline Williams. He was a student at the seminary and worked when he was not in school. I was thrilled to find that baking delicious yeast bread was among his many talents. I had never mastered this chore and was more than willing to yield this to him. It was a real treat to come home from work and find those lovely loaves of bread on the table. He would also use ripe bananas to bake wonderful banana bread. After a hard day at the office, how I praised God for these blessings. His talents made it possible for me to work eight hours at the office and still have guests for supper.

We had problems with our well pump much of the time. We would be without water and often were without lights. I learned to recycle water. We never poured out our water after bathing. It was used to mop floors or flush commodes.

It was a pleasure to have Billy Oliver as my supervisor. Cecil Williams had requested that a new filing system be set up while he was away, and the treasurer also asked if I would set up a new bookkeeping system. I saw many ways the work there could be simplified for those who would follow me. A lovely young Tanzanian girl, Lucia, worked in the office and was a tremendous help to me.

I thoroughly enjoyed working with the seminary president, Douglas Waruta. He was always so appreciative. One morning during chapel he introduced me. He talked so long that I did not understand all he said. My Swahili was not very fluent. Afterward, the other missionaries told me he had explained to the students that I was paying my own expenses to travel, live, and work in Tanzania. From that point on, the nationals treated me with an expression of awe and reverence. They could not understand why anyone who lived in America could possibly want to come to Tanzania, paying their own way! When asked by students why I came, I could only explain to them, "*Mungu anakupenda, na nina kupenda pia!*" ("God loves you, and I love you too!").

Daily, I realized how important the seminary was. We had about 80 missionaries in Tanzania, to reach 19 million citizens. Alone, it would be impossible to attain the Southern Baptist Bold Mission Thrust goal of reaching every person in the entire world by the year A.D. 2000. By training those seminary students and sending them back to their homes with the gospel, it was possible. It was a real eye-opener for me to see how God was working it all out, and I praised His name.

One special pleasure of working at the seminary was using the library. Throughout the years missionaries had come and gone, leaving their books for the library. I probably read 50 missionary biographies, including biographies about such marvelous personalities as William Carey, David Livingstone, Oswald Chambers, Charles H. Spurgeon, Albert Schweitzer, Bill Wallace, and Hudson Taylor. How I enjoyed those books.

While at the seminary I taught a class at the Greek boarding school. I asked if any seminary students would like to assist me, and so I began with two or three assistants. Before my term was over, I had a truck full of students wanting to go with me to my class. As we worked through this period, I realized that the assistants were learning, too, even though the lessons were taught at a child's level. The lessons were simple enough that the students were able to take these messages back home and put them to use. I praised the Lord!

After Lee Ray and Beth Greene returned to the States, we were without a pastor for the Arusha English Church. Attendance declined until only 10 or 12 were present for each service. If a missionary was in town, he would substitute; but on Sundays when we had no guest, I was asked to preach. I was already leading the singing, so I did the best I could.

God's protection was an amazing miracle. I had no promise when I left home that I would not find myself in a fiery furnace or a lion's den. I was only promised, "And, Eunice, I will be with you even to the end of the world." That was all I needed. God also said He would give His angels charge over me. Other missions personnel dealt with robberies, break-ins, and shootings; but your prayers called on God to keep me safe. He did.

I was awakened late one night with my bed shaking sideways. The power was off, so I got my flashlight and looked all around my room, even under my bed, and found nothing. I knew that sometimes large birds would come down the chimney, but there were none there. I lay back down and it began again. Finally it grew quiet and I fell asleep.

I was sick with a cold that weekend, so I had not made plans to go to Sunday School the next morning. About 9:00 A.M. Billy Oliver knocked on my door. He wanted to check on me before going to church. He asked if I had felt the earthquake. So, that's what it was!

My second Christmas in Africa was nearing, and I was delighted when a precious couple, Orville and Esther Beth Rogers, accepted my invitation to come and spend Christmas week with me. Orville was our volunteer pilot, and their niece, Liz, was going to be with them for the holidays. We made plans to tour Lake Manyara and also to visit the Ngorongoro Crater. We saw seven lions in one tree at Lake Manyara and many lions with their cubs at the crater. We spent one night at the Gibbses' farm and one night at a hotel. We were to be back home on Christmas Eve; but because of many flat tires on the touring van, we would not make it. Each time we had to stop and repair a flat, we sang Christmas carols. We sang from 2:00 P.M. to 9:00 P.M. We finally talked our tour guide into taking us to a hotel. We then prayed there would be room at the inn. We arrived in time to be assigned the last two rooms! And the tour guide convinced them to leave the dining room open so we could eat. God was our provider!

If I ever have to be stranded again, I want it to be with Orville, Esther Beth, and Liz! After a hot bath and a good night's rest, we met the tour van early on Christmas morning. The driver had all the flats fixed. We arrived home at 11:30 A.M. and were supposed to have our dishes ready for Christmas dinner at 2:00 P.M. I had baked cake layers and frozen them. I took them out and iced them with coconut while I tried to thaw and bake the ham.

Ed and Nancy Giddens were having the dinner at their home. Her parents were visiting from Hawaii. It was a very special time. Again, I was amazed that I never became homesick or despondent. I was too busy. I never thought I would make it through a second Christmas away from my family. My home was decorated with all the lovely cards from home, and it was a very happy occasion. God is so sufficient.

As my days in Tanzania neared an end, the Mission planned a get-together for Saturday, April 16, 1983. I was presented material for a lovely Tanzanian gown from the Mission and many other lovely gifts from individuals. The seminary gave me two lovely paintings by Tanzanian artists. It was a very special time for me. I had come to love the missionaries and nationals, and knew that I was leaving a part of my heart. I was comfortable in knowing I had given my very best in everything I had attempted. Ed Giddens and Billy Oliver were to take care of the bookkeeping at the seminary until the Williamses returned.

God was so good to let me have these experiences. Over and over it came to my mind what a risk taker God was. I could have fallen flat on my face anywhere along the way, but God was my refuge and strength. There were many surprises, but there was always the glorious assurance that whatever was happening, God was in complete control. I praised His name every step of the way. It never ceased to amaze me, that God chose me—at my age—just a bookkeeper—for such a remarkable experience.

I had not realized how much the scarcity of items in Tanzania had changed me until I started home. For instance, in the United States, we can depend on city water to be there and to be clean. We expect to flip a switch and have the lights come on, or the stove to turn on. We go to a service station and expect gasoline. Believe me, it is not like that in other parts of the world. When you spend time away from America, you return with a much greater appreciation for the way God has blessed this country.

In that lovely, huge plane from Kilimanjaro to Amsterdam, they probably served a meal each hour. With each meal I was given a large, beautiful, soft paper napkin. Each time I would gently fold my napkin and save it when I was finished. In a short time they would bring another meal and another gorgeous, absorbent, soft paper napkin. By the time we reached Amsterdam, I had a big stack of napkins.

A friend said, "You may as well throw them away. You can't save them all."

It broke my heart to throw away anything. After I arrived home and saw my church throwing away large, sectioned paper plates, I stood at the garbage can and cried. My pastor put his arms around me and tried to console me. After all, I had been in a country where no paper goods were available.

Our flight left Kilimanjaro airport at 8:35 A.M., April 19, 1983, and we spent the night in Amsterdam. We arrived in Atlanta, Georgia, on April 20 at 4:50 P.M. and finally in Birmingham, Alabama, at 8:30 P.M. My watch read 5:30 A.M. the following morning. The longest time of the whole trip was the four-hour layover in Atlanta.

I knew that in addition to all I had left behind 19 months ago, I was to meet my newest grandson. All during the trip home I had prayed, *Lord, please don't let Michael be afraid of me. I'll take care of the rest.* When I arrived at the Birmingham airport they were all there—my family, A. L. and Myra Courtney, Ida Florence Lee, and many other friends. They all stood back as Frank brought that precious 14-month-old grandson to me and said, "Michael, this is Grandmother." Michael came to me immediately and we all cried. God had kept His promise to take care of me. He had brought me back safely. Even though I looked like the wreck of the *Hesperus*, they were all glad to see me. There was not a dry eye in the airport that night.

I have told God daily I would not take a million dollars for these precious experiences. He is so great. Yes, I had wanted to go into Kenya to get my hair done before coming home, but it had not worked out as I had planned. After living in Africa for 19 months and cutting my own hair, you can imagine the first thing I did after getting home. My gracious hair stylist, Linda Hollis, took me the very next morning and repaired the damage. I was most grateful.

9

Recouping, Restoring, and Refreshing

"The Lord is my shepherd; I shall not want. He maketh me to lie down in green pastures: he leadeth me beside the still waters. He restoreth my soul: he leadeth me in the paths of righteousness for his name's sake" (Psalm 23:1–3).

After getting my hair back to normal, my second greatest need was warmer clothing. I had sold nearly all the clothes I had taken to Tanzania. I wanted to give the clothing away, but the missionaries explained that this would make enemies rather than friends. If I could not give to all, some would feel hurt, so it was better to put small prices on the items and sell them.

I had arrived home on Wednesday, and by Saturday, I was ready for some warmer clothes. My devotional that day had read, *Be ready for the sudden surprise visits from God.* After I finished my quiet time, I decided to check my cedar chest. I was surprised to find my tan pants suit, a pink wool suit, red knit dress, and much more. I could not believe it. I had forgotten I had not taken any of my warm clothes to Africa. I was so excited I ran in and woke Frances and John to tell them we did not need to go anywhere. I had plenty of clothes.

I had written home earlier in the year and asked if anyone in Pell City had an apartment I could use for an indefinite period of time. A lovely woman in our church, Margaret Mongold, responded that she had a basement apartment and would love for me to use it. This was a delight. All I needed was a place to rest between speaking engagements. On my first weekend home Frank came from Birmingham; he, John, and my grandsons moved me into Margaret's apartment. I would live there for the next six months.

It would be impossible to share all the things that took place while I was home. In addition to spending time with my family and getting to know my new grandson, I learned that furlough time for missionaries is not rest time. Even though it was April and the Week of Prayer for Foreign Missions was not until the fall, I had immediate invitations to churches, schools, civic clubs, etc. Many of the precious church families that had been especially involved in praying for me invited me to come and share with them how God had answered their prayers.

Philadelphia Baptist Church in Birmingham, Alabama, was always one of the very first places I went. I had been a charter member there before moving to Pell City. To all of those special churches that had named a missions organization after me, I had to go and express my appreciation.

As I visited with my family in Athens, Georgia, I always shared with their church, making many new friends. I also made a trip to Marshall, Texas, to visit with dear friends, Dave and Neva Milligan, sharing with their church.

Whenever I traveled more than 50 miles and would be returning the same night, I always asked someone to accompany me. Two very special friends, Ida Florence Lee and Margaret Mongold, sat through many of these presentations. I wondered if they ever got tired of hearing it over and over, but they insisted they learned something new each time.

Culver Lee and his wife, Jackie, also went along on some of my trips, saying they would take me anywhere in the US, but they would stop at the shore. Jim and Anna Laney were also very diligent to accompany me. They were all so dear.

Never in my wildest dreams did I think so many people would have an interest in what I had done. When I met my brother for lunch at his job one day, I learned that everyone in his office knew about me. He invited some of them to go to lunch with us, and, of course, I had much rather talk than eat. I enjoyed every one of them.

As soon as I saw my former employer, John Fisher, he scheduled a time for me to come and show my slides at Prairie Tank. His employees had given me the camera, and Mike Reinhardt and his wife had provided the film. We met on Thursday night, May 26, at the home of Alan and Brenda Gillison. Many employees had come from out of town. We enjoyed a wonderful dinner and a lovely time of sharing. After the slides were shown, I was asked what the trip had cost. I told them it had cost $11,400 for 19 months.

Mike said, "That last slide was worth all of it wasn't it?"

It was a slide showing the last lesson at the clinic when 16 people had accepted Christ as Savior. One friend remarked that more people had been touched by my trip than I would ever know. The truth was that I would not have traded those experiences for a million dollars.

It has never ceased to amaze me that God does call, and does use plain, ordinary people to become involved in His kingdom work. It also amazes other people too as I found out in the 110 groups I shared with that year.

One very special week I was asked to participate at a Woman's Missionary Union (WMU) leadership conference at Shocco Springs Baptist Conference Center in Talladega, Alabama. All week the attendants had been able to go to a few conferences. My room had been overflowing from the beginning. Saturday afternoon was to be our free time. Some of the women went to Mary Essie Stephens, the executive director of Alabama WMU at that time, and asked if I could do an extra session that afternoon. She asked, and I was delighted. The room was packed with people, even the missionaries whom I never did get to hear, were there. Tom and Gloria Thurman, missionaries on the roster that week, were there too. After the session, Tom said that when someone would ask him what they could do in the cause of missions he told them to go and hear Eunice Perryman and they would find their answer. That week was heaven-sent. The time spent with the missionaries and staff was so special. I came to love Mary Essie Stephens as a dear sister.

Many happy experiences took place during my trips. As one child came into the church and saw all the tables loaded with my show-and-tell items, she exclaimed, "Mother, they are having a yard sale!"

Another youngster asked what my necklace was. I told her it was ivory. She said, "Soap?" I explained that it came from an elephant tusk.

At one presentation at a boys ranch, I was asked what I missed most while I was in Africa. My immediate response was, "mayonnaise." I did not have a blender and was never able to get mayonnaise to taste right. Then I had to explain that we had to make our own mayonnaise, ketchup, mustard, buns, and even grind up the meat in order to have a hamburger. Our children here at home could not imagine. The looks on their faces were priceless.

My delight has been to share with children in any meeting. Many of the missionaries had shared with me that their first impression of God calling them to missions was felt in age-level missions groups such as Mission Friends, Royal Ambassadors, Girls in Action, and Acteens. I kept this in mind every time I spoke to children. Larry Scales once said that he remembered a missionary coming to his church who let them touch her show-and-tell items. Most missionaries had said, "Look, but don't touch." I made it a practice to let children touch whatever I had on display. I never displayed anything too fragile for them to touch.

10

Beyond My Wildest Dream

"And thine ears shall hear a word behind thee, saying, This is the way, walk ye in it" (Isa. 30:21).

I remember so clearly how God shared with me that the Dominican Republic was my next assignment. Frances Gordon of the Volunteers in Missions Department of the Foreign Mission Board (FMB) had called to say that there was no request for a bookkeeper but there was an urgent request for a secretary. Since shorthand is not one of my most capable abilities, I did not think this was for me; but she assured me shorthand was not a requirement. I asked for time to pray about it.

About two weeks later I awoke around 3:00 A.M. and was talking to the Lord. I explained that it had been two weeks and if the need was urgent, I needed His answer. As clear a sound as I have ever heard came. It was a still, small voice saying, "This is the way, walk in it!" That's all I needed. As soon as my pastor got to his office that morning, I went to share this with him. He said, "You know that is Scripture?" I had not thought about that. He picked up his Bible and read to me from Isaiah 30:21. We were assured that this was God's answer to my direction.

I called the FMB immediately and asked if this request had been filled.

Frances Gordon so graciously replied, "No, we were waiting on you!"

How marvelous is the way God works all things together. It was hard to believe God was sending me to the Caribbean. That must be like heaven. And I was willing to go back to Africa. So few were willing to go because it was hard living there. God was in control and guiding, and I thanked Him.

I had asked the family living at my farm to let me have the house as soon as their lease was up. In October 1983, I had gotten enough furniture to move into the house and lived there until going to the Dominican Republic in April 1984.

The last weekend at home before leaving, all of my family came for Sunday dinner. John Jr. asked me earlier in the day if I had any plans for the evening. I told him that other than church that night I had no plans. He and Frances wanted to talk with me privately. When everyone had gone they told me that they wanted to buy my farm. I immediately declined their offer thinking they were doing it just to help me out. They assured me this was not true. They wanted to rent from me until they could sell their home and then they would buy the farm from me. They went on to explain they had always wanted a farm just like this one. I loved the farm and this meant it would still be in the family. It had been on the market four years and never sold. Oh, the gentleness of God! Now I understood why the farm had not sold. He had kept it for my family. Every step on this journey I could see God's hand as He so beautifully placed every thread together in the tapestry of these experiences.

There had been many problems getting a visa, taking from December 1983 to April 1984 to obtain it. Even then it was only a visitor visa. We continued to work on it until we finally obtained a business visa.

I was thrilled when the plane landed in the Dominican Republic on Saturday, April 14, 1984, to see several of our missionaries and their families waiting for me. I could not learn all of their names in one evening, but they were delightful. They all escorted me on the one-hour drive along the beautiful Caribbean Sea to my lovely apartment. It was a very comfortable, beautifully furnished, third-floor apartment. There were groceries enough for a week, and on the counter was the most luscious, mellow pineapple I had ever seen. It was hard to believe what I was seeing. After all, I had thought that God would take me back to Africa. He had placed me in the Caribbean.

God had a very choice group of missionaries there. Ron Wilson was to be my supervisor. He and his wife, Janice, and their four children, Ron Jr., Anna, Timothy, and John were to become my very own family. Ron was the director of religious education in the Caribbean. I could not have asked for a more delightful and dedicated person with whom to work. Art and Martha Haylock were to be co-workers in the office. They would become dear friends and associates. While I was in the Dominican Republic, I do not believe that the Wilsons or the Haylocks ever went to the grocery store without asking me to go along. Since I did not have a vehicle much of the time, this was greatly appreciated.

The day after I arrived I had expected to go to an English church, but Danny Broskie and his wife, Brenda, and two sons, took me to Mata Hambre Church, which was Spanish-speaking. I loved every minute of it. The pastor asked Danny to introduce me. I couldn't tell you what he said because it was all in Spanish. I gave them greetings from the States, as Danny interpreted for me. The congregation then greeted me with waves and smiles. Of course, I cried.

I immediately started trying to learn some Spanish. They all laughed with me at my feeble attempts. But people everywhere love you for trying to speak their language, and love is a universal language. Yes, God is so good to let me share in His work. I really praised God for the victory there is in Jesus. He was letting me be a part of His work.

My first week in the Dominican Republic fell during Holy Week, which was celebrated the week leading up to Easter Sunday. The largest percentage of people there were Catholic. They celebrated Holy Week by not working. No one worked during that week. I was told that most Catholics there only celebrated the week to get a week off from work. What a shame that to so many people Easter means nothing more than that. Most of them had no relationship with the Christ of the cross.

The views from my apartment windows were gorgeous. From the front I could see the city with beautiful mountains rising up behind it. From the rear I could see the city with the Caribbean Sea stretching out before it. I asked the Lord many times if He was sure He wanted me in the Caribbean.

Santo Domingo was gorgeous. Beautiful apartment buildings, large stores, supermarkets, and fruit stands lined the streets. My, what a treat! Ron, Janice, and the children took me to the supermarkets and then to a huge market where crafts, coral, and souvenirs were for sale. I saw so many things I wanted to buy for show-and-tell before going back to the States. Prices were much less than I had expected. I learned immediately that I could get a chicken for only $2. I also learned that one of Ron Wilson's favorite foods was chicken and dumplings. I knew I would be cooking lots of that!

My second week was hectic. We went into the office thinking we would be able to get a full week's work accomplished. Shortly after we arrived our young helper came back from town and advised us all to go home, get inside, and stay there. He said there was a revolution beginning in town. Just 30 minutes away people were burning tires in the streets, blocking traffic, setting a bus on fire, and doing lots of shouting and rioting because the president had raised prices. It would not be safe for us to be out. Foreign missionaries never participate in politics, so we all stayed home and kept a very low profile for more than a week.

We bought enough groceries to last several days before going home. It was upsetting to come out of the market with our baskets loaded, only to see the nationals with only one or two items, mostly red beans and rice. Our missionaries are on a cost-of-living index, so if prices are raised, they are not hurt as much as the nationals. When we pray for our missionaries, we are not always aware of their situations, but we need to lift them up in prayer. Always.

God gave me some of the most precious moments at totally unexpected times. I received a card one day from the Alagasco Bible Study, the gas company in Birmingham where my brother, Richard Harris, was a manager. I was not aware that they had a Bible study there. The card was filled with small notes and signatures. One man wrote, "We are praying that you will be filled with His mighty, glorious strength, so that you can keep going, no matter what happens and that you will always be full of the joy of the Lord" (Col. 1:11). He would never know how much I needed that prayer.

The office of our Baptist Mission was only one mile from my apartment. I did not have a vehicle. God gave me an opportunity to get some exercise, morning and night. I sometimes walked home for lunch, but it was much easier to take my lunch and stay out of the midday heat. The transportation system consisted of very small cars called *publicos*. They usually carried six to eight people. Because I didn't know how to tell them to let me off, I continued to walk until I finally made up my mind to try it. The cars would not come to a complete stop. A rider would just walk out from the curb, the *publico* would slow down, a door would open, and you just sort of fell in. If there was room, you got a seat; if not, you just squeezed in, or sat on someone.

My first attempt to tell them where I wanted to get off came out in a slow, southern drawl, *"Casa Bautista Publicaciones."* Everyone in the car laughed with me while I held out my hand with some coins in it. The cost of the ride is determined by the distance you ride. One of the men took some coins, so I knew what it would cost me the next time. When the driver came near my exit, I started saying, *"Aquí"* ("here"), so he pulled over and let me fall out. What an experience!

I also had problems answering the phone at work. Since most of the people calling spoke Spanish, I had to listen very carefully. If I heard the words, *"Señor Ronaldi,"* I knew they wanted Ron Wilson; *"Señor Arturo"* meant they wanted Art Haylock. If I couldn't understand anything they were saying, I said, *"Un momento, por favor,"* meaning "one moment, please," put them on hold, and yelled for help.

I started studying Spanish two afternoons a week. At age 64, learning a new language was not easy, but the nationals seemed to appreciate my feeble attempts to learn. I had not asked God for an easy task. My biggest satisfaction came when I was able to sing "Because He Lives" in Spanish. It is still a delight.

One day I decided to catch a ride from the office to the market. When I had finished my shopping I took my bag of groceries and waited at the corner for the *publico*. A downpour began, and because I had not brought an umbrella, I stood under a business canopy for about 30 minutes waiting for it to stop. I finally ventured out to get a *publico*.

When I got in the front seat, there was already another passenger and the driver, so I made the third person on that seat. The window was out on my side, and it started to rain again. The woman in the middle got out and I moved to the center when another passenger got in. The driver handed him a rag because he was soaked. The man took the rag and put it between me and him.

We hit a puddle in the road. The car must have had no bottom because water came up through the floorboard and in through the window. When I finally arrived home and went into the bathroom to get a shower, what a sight I was. I got so tickled. I remembered Clyde Dotson's message the night I was commissioned. He had challenged, "Sit where they sit." Well, let me tell you, I had really fulfilled that challenge. If one should ever want to get close to the people, just let them ride the *publico*. Right then and there I appreciated knowing someone was praying for me so that I could keep on going, no matter what came my way. Thank you for those prayers.

11

Mission Hostess

"Use hospitality one to another without grudging"
(1 Peter 4:9).

One of the greatest delights in all my trips was having guests in my home. Because my apartment had three bedrooms, any missionary coming to Santo Domingo from another area stayed with me. Dan and Betty Alice Carroll came from El Paso, Texas, to fill in for the Broskies as literature administrator while Danny and his family went home on furlough. While the Carrolls were getting acquainted with their new job, they stayed with me. When the Broskies left, the Carrolls moved into their home. I really enjoyed having them with me. They had served in Argentina, Jamaica, and for the last 11 years, at the Spanish Publishing House in El Paso, Texas. Betty Alice had edited and written Sunday School lessons, translating from Greek to Spanish.

Every time missionaries were in my home it was a pleasure to serve the local fruits, pineapples, papayas, cantaloupes, bananas, and mangoes. They were so delicious. The Dominican Republic is so blessed with wonderful fruits. We served them with meals and enjoyed them all day long as well.

Our Mission meeting was planned for June 17–22, 1984, at the Montemar Hotel in Puerto Plata on the northern coast. This was a real treat for me. We would travel the four-hour drive in vans, and I would be able to see the Dominican Republic from the southern coast to the northern coast.

On Sunday, June 17, the Foreign Mission Board (FMB) associate area director, Bill Graves, and his wife, Marjorie; and then FMB vice-president, Bill O'Brien, and his wife, Dellanna, were coming for our Mission meeting. Since I was not teaching Sunday School, I volunteered to prepare lunch. Afterward we would leave for Puerto Plata. It was delightful. I baked ham with all the scrumptious fruits around it. I also made fried chicken, potato salad, gelatin salad, chocolate pound cake, and more. I prepared most of it on Saturday.

Roger Gaunt and family came in that night needing a place to stay. I was delighted to host them. On Sunday morning, the Graveses, O'Briens, Haylocks, Wilsons, Carrolls, Teels, and the Gaunts were there for lunch. We were all so amused when Dellanna O'Brien could not bear to leave the fruits and asked for a doggie bag to take the leftovers.

Just before leaving for the Mission meeting I had received a letter from the Mission administrator in Tanzania, Jim Houser. He said they had requested another Eunice Perryman from the FMB to fill in for Roger Swann during his furlough beginning August 1985. He asked if it would be possible for me to come back. I had no idea what God had in store for me because He never pulls the shade in advance, but it was certainly a compliment to be invited back.

The Mission meeting was a very high time spiritually, as well as a time of wonderful fellowship. I thought that volunteers might not be included in the meetings, but I was included in every session. On Wednesday, Martha Haylock, who was serving as Mission secretary, came down with a virus and was very sick. When she had to drop out from taking the minutes, I stepped in to fill the gap. Can you imagine taking minutes for a business meeting eight to ten hours each day?

Each night we enjoyed a devotional time with Bill O'Brien leading and singing. He sang a special song he had written for the foreign missions emphasis, "Because He First Loved Us." Hearing him sing it was worth the whole week. When those God has called come together to plan their work and goals and seek out His will for their work, it is a very special time.

When you are aware a Mission is having its annual meeting, please pray. Those missionaries want more than anything else in all the world to follow God's will for their Mission.

At the close of the Mission meeting, I had taken a cold. I had not been accustomed to the air-conditioning at the Montemar Hotel. On Sunday morning I did not go to church. I was sitting in my rocking chair just praising God for bringing me to the Dominican Republic when all at once I felt the apartment building begin to shake. My chair was rocking sideways. Looking out the windows I saw no wind blowing. The shaking lasted about 20 seconds. Five minutes later, a small flutter began, but not as hard as the first. Everyone in the apartment complex came out into the courtyard in their pajamas and began dancing and singing. Later I learned that the earthquake had registered 6.5 on the Richter Scale. It had demolished one building and killed four people. My concern was that these precious people had seemingly no thought about their spiritual conditions. My prayer was that God would use me to make a difference in their lives.

From the time I arrived in the Dominican Republic I had been puzzled why none of the missionaries ever went fishing. All that beautiful water was just going to waste. Since they had made me Mission hostess, I felt I should do something about this. I kept mentioning fishing until finally they relented, saying if I would make the arrangements, they would go. That's all I needed! I immediately called and reserved one of the boats. It would only hold 8, so I reserved another one. We had 16 people ready to go. The water was choppy that morning, which contributed to much sickness on both boats. The captain said we could turn back and let the sick ones off, but it would limit the distance we would be able to travel. We decided to go back and let the sick ones out. There were 3 on one boat and 5 on the other. The rest of us went fishing.

Ron Wilson Jr. caught the first fish, and this was his first fishing trip. We caught some real beauties and enjoyed the trip immensely. I caught a dolphin about 30 inches long. All of the men fishing were preachers, but there was not a fisherman in the group. They teased me for catching the biggest fish. It was a very special occasion. Fishing had always been one of my favorite pastimes. After all, God said in Genesis 1:28, "And God blessed them, and God said unto them . . . have dominion over the fish of the sea." You guessed it, they never did let me plan another fishing trip.

I continued to entertain guests. Don Kammerdiener, our area director at that time, came for several days. Ron gave me the morning off and I prepared lunch for all our missionaries. We enjoyed baked ham, chicken and dumplings, sweet potato casserole (I had to put food coloring in this because the potatoes were white), green beans, slaw, fruit salad, and fresh coconut cake. Needless to say, I had adopted all the missionaries.

The next day Roger Gaunt came in from San Juan de la Maguana, and invited me out to lunch. I suggested we eat leftovers at my apartment. He said, "No." He wanted to take me out. The other missionaries began to tell him what he would be missing, so yes, we ate leftovers.

My 64th birthday came while I was there. The missionaries made the whole week special. One couple took me to a Chinese restaurant for lunch on Sunday. Another couple took me to a French restaurant for crepes then to an Italian ice-cream store for dessert. That night I was heating a bowl of soup for supper when Dan Carroll came in. He said he was in the doghouse with Betty Alice because he was supposed to have invited me to have supper with them. He asked if I would please put the soup in the refrigerator. They took me to Piccolo's, a lovely Italian Restaurant with live music. Tuesday night the Haylocks picked me up and took me to the Wilsons' for a surprise birthday party! The children had made very special gifts. Everyone was so dear. They insisted I take the lovely flowers and remaining cake home with me. A call from Pell City made my birthday even more special. My family called from home to sing "Happy Birthday." A. L. and Myra Courtney also called to assure me that my church family was holding the ropes in prayer. How I thank my heavenly Father for the family of God all over the world!

In the fall of 1984 I was asked if I planned on going home for Christmas. I was not aware that volunteers were allowed to do this. I was elated and asked them to make the arrangements. Ron Wilson made a recommendation to the executive board that they allow me a 30-day holiday for Christmas. I immediately contacted the Volunteers in Missions Department of the FMB and obtained permission. I also requested that my stay in the Dominican Republic be extended from April 1985 to September 1985 when the Wilsons were to go on furlough.

On December 8, 1984, I left to spend a month at home with family and friends. What a wonderful Christmas that was. I had to turn down invitations to speak at churches because my time was so short. However, I did share with my church on December 9. At the close of the Week of Prayer for Foreign Missions observance we watched our offering climb to meet our goal of $10,000 and then exceed it. God was evident in so many ways during this furlough. When my former employer, John Fisher, learned I had no transportation, he called me and said, "There is a car waiting on you here in our yard! May I deliver it?" I praised God from Whom all blessing flow! My every need was provided above all I could ask or even think.

The Sam Shaw family, missionaries in Santiago, Dominican Republic, had a terrible wreck while I was home on furlough. They were on their way to the home of David Dupree where they were to have Christmas dinner. Their collision totaled their vehicle. Sam fractured four vertebrae, and Ruthie had multiple broken bones and was in very bad condition. Corrie and Joey had some broken bones, but the oldest and the youngest of the children were spared any broken bones.

All members of the Mission family were called into action and stayed around the clock with them. The collision occurred on Christmas Eve. On December 29, the FMB sent an airplane from Florida with medics and nurses on board to fly them to a hospital in Tulsa, Oklahoma, so they could be near their family. Sam and Ruthie had been preparing to leave on furlough in January, so most of their things were packed.

When I returned after the holidays, James and Georgie Teel had been transferred to their new station in Canada. The mission had approved me to drive the Teels' vehicle. Now I could go the market and drive to church. I was immediately able to help a missionary in distress. Danny Broskie had let the others use his van to ship the freight home to the Shaw family. He had no way to get home for lunch or to pick up his children from school. I said, "No problem. I'll be right there." When he thanked me, I shared that my service to them had been limited by my not having a vehicle. I surely could not bake a cake and take it by *publico* to anyone!

During one of our holidays, I had enjoyed doing my favorite thing—baking. I baked an apple pie and a fresh coconut cake and then wished for someone to help me eat them. About 7:00 P.M. my doorbell rang. Several of the male missionaries from the media conference had come by. Paul Siebenmann from Puerto Plata, David Dupree from La Vega, Roger Gaunt from San Juan de la Maguana, and two national pastors, Manola Sarita, president of the national convention, and Pablo Sanchez, a former president of the convention, stood at my door. Paul offered the excuse that he wanted me to tell them about Africa, but they had eaten their supper and were really just looking for dessert! I was delighted to serve them. When we all had finished, there was one piece of pie and one piece of cake left. I guess we left that for the sake of manners! "But Martha was cumbered about much serving" (Luke 10:40). *Lord, don't ever let me place serving as a first priority, but You really did give me the gift of serving, and I thank You for that.*

My supervisor, Ron Wilson, was serving at that time as chairman of the Christian Education/Stewardship Committee of the Caribbean Baptist Fellowship. The fellowship consisted of all the islands in the Caribbean and three countries on the northern coast of South America. About 60 percent of his time was spent in that capacity, and the other 40 percent as director of religious education and evangelism. I enjoyed preparing all of his materials and putting them in order for his workshops. I learned shortly after arriving that Janice was never able to participate in these workshops with him because of their four children. I immediately offered to stay with the children so Janice could go. They had an excellent maid and cook, so my major responsibility was loving the children and seeing them to bed each night. Ron Jr. and Anna were a great help. They would bathe the two smaller ones and did most everything that was needed. I did what I do best; I was the grandmother. I loved every minute of it. Sometimes Ron and Janice's plane schedules did not work as planned, but they always knew I would stay until they returned.

The English church had a Spanish group and also a Chinese group. They alternated for the use of the auditorium and the Sunday School rooms. Once I was asked to substitute teach a youth class. We had two present the first Sunday. The next Sunday we had seven. I saw a real opportunity to reach out; and knowing there was no teacher for the group, I asked the pastor if I might keep that class. We were located very close to the high school and there was a tremendous opportunity to reach those young people. The pastor said, "No." He did not approve of a woman teaching a class with young boys in it. That was the end of the youth class. This broke my heart. It was my first experience in meeting with this attitude. Everywhere I had been God had affirmed my working with boys, girls, men, and women. I loved them all, but I had to back off and leave the situation in God's hands.

Art and Martha Haylock took me to hear a concert by José Garcia, a great concert soloist and artist. Even though it was all in Spanish, I enjoyed every bit of it. José was really preaching the gospel in song. His grand finale was drawing a picture as he sang. He was a terrific artist. When he was called to pastor the Quisqueya Baptist Church, I knew this was where I would be going.

I started attending the Spanish Quisqueya Church when I returned after Christmas. The services were so outstanding. I would study the sermon from my Spanish-English Bible, and if I knew the songs they sang in Spanish, I would just sing them in English.

José and his wife, Mayra, enjoyed dropping by my apartment. José spoke beautiful English and Mayra spoke some.

My afternoon classes in Spanish really helped. My teacher was a Cuban refugee and was very interested in what I was doing. We would talk a lot about Africa. One day she asked what I would have done if I had gotten sick while in Africa. I answered that the same God who took me to Africa also made my body. She just shook her head.

Paul and Peggy Siebenmann were having a Baptist Student Union witnessing team come from Puerto Rico for a unique beach ministry. Peggy asked me if I would like to come up that week to Puerto Plata and help cook for the 15 young people and the Siebenmann family of 5. I went and it was a very special week. I served as houseparent to the young women. We stayed in a missionary journeyman's apartment. The young men stayed at the church. Of course, anyone who wandered in at mealtime ate with us, so we never knew how many there would be. At noon we packed sandwiches and went to the beach. At night everyone came in from the beach, bathed, ate, and then went to the church for revival services.

Revival services were very different from what I was accustomed to in the States. They were scheduled to begin at 7:00 P.M., but never began until 8:00 P.M., with people usually still arriving at 8:30 P.M. Our evangelist, Jorge Diaz, actually got started around 8:45 P.M. and preached until way after 10:00 P.M. There were professions made every night—the fruit of the beach ministry.

On our last night in Puerto Plata, the doorbell rang about 2:00 A.M. One of the girls got up to answer the door and I was right behind her. We had a rule of no boys in our apartment. A group of men had come to serenade us. Among the men were Paul Siebenmann, Manola Sarita, and all the young men working with the ministry. They sang for about an hour. Afterward we served them cold drinks. I began to wonder if these people ever slept. I was going home the next day, so all was well. *Thank You, Lord, for happy, precious, appreciative people.* Now I can honestly say, "I've been serenaded." It was just one more of my very special experiences.

All these experiences were fringe benefits because God carried me to the Dominican Republic to do secretarial work. He did not say that was all I could do. It was only when I was willing to be involved in other areas that God really poured out His blessings! I praised Him every day for bringing me to the Dominican Republic.

For those of you who use the prayer calendar to pray for missionaries on their birthdays, let me share with you that it is the most special day for them. Ron Wilson's birthday drew near and I was invited to come for his birthday supper. Janice had prepared a delicious supper and the children were so anxious for their dad to open his presents. As he started to open one, 4-year-old John said, "I bet it is some little cars!"

Ron asked, "For what?"

John said, "Everyone wants some little cars to play with!"

We all had a good laugh at that. Just as we were ready to cut the cake a woman from their church arrived with an ice-cream cake, three layers thick! Janice put the candles on it, we sang "Happy Birthday," and he blew out his candles. Then we dove into the desserts. The highlight of his birthday came when he opened a card from their home church in the States. It informed him that a car was waiting on them at the missionary residence where they would live while on furlough. Ron really did get his little car!

The nationals enjoy all our holidays. On Mother's Day (which is on a different day there) in 1984 I was invited to a Chinese home for dinner. This was a special treat. In 1985 my pastor, José, and his wife, Mayra, invited me to spend Mother's Day with them. His invitation was so precious. He said, "We know you will be away from your children, and the missionaries would have you spend it with them, but we really would like to have you with us on Mother's Day." I cried, of course, hugged them, and graciously accepted their invitation.

It was always a special treat to be invited into the homes of the nationals. José, Mayra, and I enjoyed such an easy cama-raderie. It was as if they were my grandchildren. We went to a port where large boats came in. There was a restaurant there which had live music. José had them play special songs for me. It was unbelievable! If anyone back home was feeling sorry for me on Mother's Day, the sympathy was wasted. I was with one of the most special couples in the world, in one of the most beautiful spots in the world, being loved, and returning that love. Talk about fringe benefits. Who could ask for anything more?

Sundays were always special. The Embajador Hotel had the most wonderful breakfast buffets. I usually went to the early church service and Sunday School. Art and Martha Haylock and I would then go enjoy the breakfast buffet. It was a gorgeous feast for an inexpensive price. Every Sunday was special because of it.

12

The Gentleness of God

"I must work the works of him that sent me, while it is day: the night cometh, when no man can work" (John 9:4).

In the spring of 1985 the question of where I would be serving next kept coming up. Wilson Donehoo, the Foreign Mission Board (FMB) treasurer for the Caribbean area, called to ask if I would be interested in going to Barbados Bible College to assist in an audit. Of course, I said yes and obtained permission from the Dominican Republic Mission.

It was a delightful trip. Eva Smith, who worked in Wilson's office, was to do the audit. Bill Womack, president of Barbados Bible College, and his wife, Elba, were gracious hosts. As soon as the audit was complete, Elba insisted on showing us around Barbados for shopping and sight-seeing. It was a very special time. When the trip was over, Wilson asked if I would come and work in this office while he and his wife, Martha, went home on furlough. I assured him I would pray about it.

I really wanted to be where God wanted me to be. The Dominican Republic executive committee had also invited me to come back and work there. I had three invitations, and I really did not know what to do. I started praying that God would make His will clear to me. The easiest thing to do would be to stay in the Dominican Republic. I had a lovely apartment and a vehicle. I knew the missionaries and the work needed. I had never asked God for an easy task, and in God's own time He made His answer very clear.

In May 1985 lots of changes were taking place. The Haylocks were going home on an early furlough because of an illness in their family. The Wilsons would be going on furlough in August. Then we learned the Broskies were expecting a new arrival. Brenda had multiple sclerosis, so the doctors advised her to go back to the States to have the baby. They would also be leaving in August. With such a big exodus the Hagewoods would be the only couple left in Santo Domingo, and there was not much work for me to do.

All the changes meant I had to make some decisions. Since half of my time was spent working with Ron Wilson and the other half with Art Haylock, I would not be needed after they left. I still did not have a definite answer from God. Ron suggested I call the FMB. Frances Gordon patiently shared that she had two requests for secretaries. One was secretary to the director of evangelism for Europe and the Middle East in Belgium and the other was secretary to the doctors in Taiwan. All my life I had wanted to go to the Orient. Frances added that they could always get secretaries, but they needed a bookkeeper in Puerto Rico. Though Puerto Rico was under the leadership of the Home Mission Board (HMB), the FMB based their personnel who oversaw the Caribbean area in that country for logistical reasons.

She said, "You are the only bookkeeper we have." That settled it. As much as I would have loved to go to Belgium or Taiwan, I wanted most to go where I was needed. I agreed to go to Puerto Rico.

Wednesday, May 29, 1985, was our monthly prayer day. There were only seven of us present; but as always, it was a special day. After lunch we all returned to the office. I had just gotten to the office when the phone rang. It was my son, John. They had sold their house and were ready to buy my farm! He wanted to know what I wanted him to do with the money for the farm. I had two options. They could have all the papers drawn up and I could fly home for one weekend to close the sale, or they could put the money in the bank and finalize the sale when I came home in two or three months. I decided to wait until I went home on furlough. I bowed my head, and through my tears, I praised God for His faithfulness and grace. Only the month before had we prayed for God's will to be done concerning the farm. Brenda Broskie had prayed that if God willed John and Frances to have the farm, He would move their house to sell. Oh, how great God is! Jesus said, "If ye abide in me, and my words abide in you, ye shall ask what ye will, and it shall be done unto you" (John 15:7). As I sat there crying, Ron and Janice came in, thinking I had received some bad news. When I shared what God had done, we all rejoiced and cried together.

One of the things I enjoyed most about living in my apartment was the children. The adults had been hesitant to have anything to do with me because I was a member of the minority race. The children did not seem to see the color of my skin, even though I was the only white-skinned person in the 54-unit complex. I quickly learned that when I started baking cookies, I could expect some of the children to show up needing help with their English. I needed help with my Spanish so we helped each other and enjoyed the cookies. It worked for Lottie Moon and it worked for me!

The children had a basketball goal on a telephone pole in the parking lot, the only place they had to play. The goal had no net. One day I passed a yard sale and spotted a net. I took it home for them. After that I never had to carry my groceries up the three flights of stairs again.

One day I heard the children playing and went to the sliding glass door to watch them. They waved at me and I waved back. One of the children called out, "Hi, Grandmother!"

I answered, "Hi, Granddarling!"

Then he called out, "I am your friend!"

With tears streaming down my face, I answered, "I am your friend also."

I had not realized how I had missed hearing the title grandmother, but God knew. My mind went to the words in Isaiah 11:6, "And a little child shall lead them."

As June approached I knew it would be a busy month. Mission meeting was scheduled for June 16–21. We had a lot of material to prepare in a very short time. As a volunteer, I also had to prepare my own report for the Mission meeting. Let me share with you some of my goals.

1. To be a true witness for God in every opportunity.
2. By my life, to show the nationals that God loves them, and I love them too.
3. To serve the church I attended in any way possible.
4. To do my work to the very best of my ability.
5. To do more than is required of me.
6. To relieve the missionaries in every way possible.
7. To keep a happy disposition in my work.

Some of the goals I had reached and in some I had seen no visible results. It continued to amaze me that God had chosen me for such a special assignment.

The dearest report I typed was a volunteer evaluation report. I told Ron I did not think I should see it, but he pleaded that no one would be able to read his writing. My grades were at the top in every category. Under "Remarks" he had written, "I could never have accomplished what I have this year, were it not for Eunice." I thanked God for that affirmation. I had sometimes felt a failure because I had not won anyone to the Lord, or even taught Sunday School. God had used what I had done and I thanked Him.

With four couples leaving in August, it was thought my job in the Dominican Republic could be completed by the end of July. This allowed four or five weeks to complete all the reports and minutes of the meeting and time to organize and distribute them. It was approved for me to return to the States at that time.

During Mission meeting I received a letter from my home church, First Baptist Church, Pell City, Alabama, telling me an apartment had been prepared for me. The church planned to furnish and keep the apartment for me so that I could come and go as God led.

When friends in Alabama learned I would be home in time for the Week of Prayer for Foreign Missions, invitations starting pouring in. I remembered that after my return from Tanzania I had spoken to 110 different groups. It was so exciting that God continued to astonish me by bringing glory to His name with what He was doing with me.

One invitation I received was from Mary Essie Stephens of Montgomery, Alabama. She had retired after serving as executive director of Alabama Woman's Missionary Union (WMU) for 30 years. She wanted me to come to Montgomery during the Week of Prayer for Foreign Missions. She and Brunies Cauthen, associational WMU director, had set up a schedule putting me at ten different churches that week. I was to be a guest in her home. It would be a very special week.

As my time in the Dominican Republic drew to an end, my heart was torn. I had come to love these people so very much. The country was beautiful. I had left a part of my heart in Tanzania, and now I was leaving another part here. Many times I would get a tight feeling in my chest knowing I might never pass this way again. When a volunteer completes a long-term assignment, the Mission often shows its appreciation with a gift. This gift was special. Peggy Siebenmann came from Puerto Plata and spent the weekend with me. She showed a great interest in my clothes (getting my size) and the embroidery work that I was doing (learning my favorite colors). She even took some of my thread home. My gift from the Mission was a beautiful ankle-length dress, orchid in color; with embroidery on the sleeves, yoke, down the front, and around the bottom. Six of the women in her church had made it!

Many more kindnesses were shown to me before I left. My last night there, José and Mayra Garcia came by, bringing a beautiful tea set made of native pottery with original designs on it. Since everything was already packed, I opened my footlocker and threw out some shoes and other nonessential items to make room for my very special tea set.

Later that evening I walked down the stairs on my way to the market for some last-minute items. There was a small, one-room grocery at the corner of my apartment complex. As I entered, a man whom I did not know introduced himself as the owner of the apartments. He said, "I understand you are going back to the States. Where is home?"

I answered, "Alabama."

He said, "I envy Alabama."

My ears perked up. I asked, "Oh, do you know about Alabama?"

He replied, "No, I don't know about Alabama. I envy Alabama because they will have you. You have made a difference in these apartments."

I thanked him, not fully understanding what he meant. The only influence I was aware of was the children I loved so much. This man never knew what his words meant to me. I had not won a single soul to the Lord while in the Dominican Republic, and I was leaving very dissatisfied. The main reason I was sent there was to witness for the Lord. I thought I had failed; but if I had made a difference, then it was all worth it.

The morning of July 27, 1985, several missionary families came to see me off. It was like leaving brothers and sisters who were very dear to me. The most touching thing was the children in the apartment complex. As I left my apartment the children were sitting along the stairway, all the way from the third floor to the ground! They were so dear and I loved them so much.

As I left the Dominican Republic, my prayer for the Baptist Mission and the nationals was Ephesians 3:16–21: "That Christ may dwell in your hearts by faith; that ye, being rooted and grounded in love, may be able to comprehend with all saints what is the breadth, and length, and depth, and height; and to know the love of Christ, which passeth knowledge, that ye might be filled with all the fullness of God. Now unto him that is able to do exceeding abundantly above all that we ask or think, according to the power that worketh in us, unto him be glory in the church by Christ Jesus throughout all ages, world without end. Amen."

There is still victory in Jesus and He is letting you and me be a part of that victory! Praise His name!

Coming home this time was very special. I was to have my very own little apartment. My church family had prepared it with lovely curtains, linens, and food. When I arrived, Bill Waller and Rudolph Miner were completing the new porch and steps leading into the apartment. They had worried about the old steps being sufficient. Their wives, Mary Nell Miner and Ruby Katherine Waller, had been working inside the apartment, along with my pastor's wife, Myra Courtney, and many others from the church. They were as excited about it as I was.

I shared my appreciation to the church the following Sunday. I told them of a beautiful hotel in the Dominican Republic which was decorated by the well-known fashion designer Oscar de la Renta. It was done in blue, green, and orchid. So was my apartment. The living and dining area was blue; the bedroom green. When I opened the cabinets, I discovered they were done in orchid. They had run out of paint and time and had used what they had. I told my church family that I probably had the only Oscar de la Renta apartment in all of Alabama. Oh, how I appreciated all of those dear friends. A very special member of my church, Millie Ann Lawley, offered me her car, and this completed my needs. God never leaves anything out when He is in control.

Again, the whirlwind of activities began. Some weeks were filled with up to 11 appearances, many of them places where I had been on my last furlough.

In addition to speaking, some of my time was spent with Pam Waddell, coauthor of this book. I am sure she felt like giving up because I had so little time to spend with her. I gave her my diaries as well as all the letters that I had written home each week. Ida Florence Lee and Betty Harris had saved every letter and had given them back to me.

In addition to the encouragement from missionaries to write my story, I received a letter from Mary Essie Stephens saying:

"You are truly one of God's marvels! Who is writing your story? It should be recorded other than in heaven, where the full script, I am sure, is being carefully set down."

After being home from July 1985 until January 1986, it was time to move on to whatever God had in store for me. That's what made it so exciting! I never knew what He had planned, but I was willing to walk by faith as He led.

13

The Computer World

"I will go before thee, and make the crooked places straight: I will break in pieces the gates of brass, and cut in sunder the bars of iron" (Isa. 45:2).

Moving into Fred and Janice Day's apartment in Puerto Rico was a new experience. Their apartment was on the 11th floor of a lovely apartment building. There was even an elevator. There were seven locks between the front gate and the apartment door. Whenever I bought groceries, I could buy only what I could carry in my arms. I had to open each lock, one at a time. I went to the store twice a day because it was only two blocks away.

The apartment complex had a tall, iron fence around the parking lot. The fence gate had to be opened by either an electronic eye or a key. The door leading into the building was locked and another door in the vestibule also stayed locked. The elevator needed another key. At my door there was an iron gate across the opening which required a key. The door itself had a dead-bolt lock and a lock in the doorknob. Using a little ingenuity, I put a ribbon on one key, nail polish on another, tape on another, etc., until I was able to remember the sequence of keys. I learned that all these locks were necessary because of the high rate of crime in Puerto Rico.

Wilson and Martha Donehoo took me to Calvary Baptist Church on my first Sunday. This church did not have a watch-care program, which would have made it easier on missionaries to be active members without actually moving their memberships from their home churches. I did not want to move my membership from First Baptist Church, Pell City; but after two or three weeks, I knew that for me to participate fully in the work there, I would need to become a member. A call home to my pastor assured me that I would always belong to the First Baptist Church family in Pell City.

Immediately after joining Calvary Baptist Church, the pastor shared a need for someone to teach a new members class. The pastor explained that he wanted me to teach six weeks on the meaning of the conversion experience, the new life in Christ, and what church membership really meant. At the end of the six weeks we were to turn each new member over to an alumnus of the Masterlife program. He or she would walk with the new member through the *New Christian Survival Kit.* They wanted a lot of emphasis placed on memorizing Scripture. As I finished with one group they hoped to have another ready to start. We had eight in the first group, ranging from college age to retirement age. I thoroughly enjoyed working with them, having them in my home, and treating them to southern hospitality and fellowship. The Baptist Women needed a program chairman. I accepted that job also. It has never ceased to amaze me that everywhere God has taken me, there were jobs just waiting for me. He knew what I could do and led me to do it.

The prices in Puerto Rico were a shock, after living in the Dominican Republic where prices were so low. I had paid only 1 peso (approximately 50¢) for a pineapple or a luscious bag of mangoes in the Dominican Republic. On my first shopping trip in Puerto Rico, I chose a pineapple and other needed items, thinking I would figure out the cost later. After figuring all the prices, I was shocked. I did not wait until later to cry. That pineapple had cost me $3.85! A pound of coffee had cost $4.97. I would have to change my way of living. Everything has to be shipped into Puerto Rico, causing very high prices. When my home church found out the difference in the cost of living, they voted to contribute to my support. They were aware I had sold the farm and God had provided, making the gesture unnecessary; but they wanted to have a part in the ministry God had called me to do. From the very beginning they had held the ropes in prayer; but now they were taking it one step further, providing $250 per quarter for a total of $1,000 during the year I was to be in Puerto Rico.

Wilson Donehoo, the Foreign Mission Board (FMB) treasurer for the Caribbean area, was to be my supervisor. He and his wife, Martha, lived in an apartment across the street from me. The office was only six blocks from there. Martha kept all the information on computer and Eva Smith worked as the bookkeeper. Wilson and Martha were preparing to leave on furlough and needed someone who could use the computer. They had hired a woman who would start in May and would assume this responsibility. The last Sunday in February she informed Wilson that she had taken another job and would not be coming to work for him. This upset all our plans. I had been playing with the computer, but to me it was a vicious animal! On one occasion I was entering our mailing list into the computer so that mailing labels could be printed, when something got onto the screen which did not belong there. It asked, *What do you want to do?* I told it to go on to the next number, but it went backward! I started talking to the machine and everyone laughed at me. It was funny until we learned that I was going to have to do the bookkeeping on that thing.

God's Word had spoken to me many years ago. Second Corinthians says, "For if there be first a willing mind, it is accepted according to that a man hath, and not according to that he hath not." I prayed, *Now, Lord, You promised that You would not call me to do something I cannot do.* He had promised to supply all my needs. Did I ever have a need!

God asked me, *Do you really have a willing mind?*

Humbly, I answered, *Yes, Lord.*

When Wilson realized it was up to us, he invited a lovely missionary angel, Janet Herbert, stationed with the media department in the Bahama Islands to come and acquaint herself with the computer program, so that while he and Martha were away, she could help, if needed. Janet took my hand, and with her patience and sweet, sweet spirit, walked me through the program. We worked together for three days. My home church knew how hesitant I was about using this computer and went into overtime praying for me. I received a letter from Myra Courtney, saying that they were praying that God would turn on the light and I would be able to understand that computer. That is exactly what God did. All at once the comprehension came, and the monster I had so hated became my dearest friend. Even though Janet was satisfied that I could do it, she assured me she was as close as a phone call.

Janet had stayed with the Wilsons while she was in Puerto Rico. Before she left, she brought a small gift by my apartment, a framed piece of cross-stitching. The message said, "My grace is sufficient for thee." It was lovely! I was so very grateful to God for letting me know Janet. That precious gift is still hanging on my bedroom wall. God is faithful to His promises. I never had to call for help during the entire time Wilson and Martha were gone. Only God could have gotten me through that year.

Getting to know the missionaries has been one of my favorite fringe benefits. Bill Graves and his wife, Marjorie, were so gracious to me. I had met them when they visited the Dominican Republic. Bill was serving as the associate area director of the Northwest Caribbean and was nearing retirement. Fred Day was associate area director of the Southeast Caribbean. With him on furlough, Bill and Marjorie really had their very capable hands full. They were a delightful couple, always ready and willing to help. Bill was very helpful in getting materials for me to use in the new members class.

One special experience for me was the Baptist Women retreat. I had not had an opportunity to get acquainted with many of the Puerto Ricans. This retreat gave me a wonderful opportunity. Two lovely women, Virginia Caughman and Betty Yarbrough, came from South Carolina to teach. I enjoyed the fellowship and sharing of what God is doing all over the world. On Sunday night Beatrice Duffer, president of the Puerto Rico Woman's Missionary Union (WMU), brought the two guests to our church service. I had the privilege of taking the three of them out to eat after church. It was a happy week-end and I hated to see them leave. It was always so good to see someone from the States.

Shortly after I arrived in Puerto Rico, I learned of a pro-gram on the cruise ships that offered reduced rates to people willing to teach arts and crafts while on the cruise. Many of the missionaries took their vacations this way. Wilson and Martha wanted Eva Smith and me to take advantage of this program before they left on furlough. I knew this would prob-ably be my only opportunity to take a cruise. We contacted the agent and signed up for a week, leaving Puerto Rico on a Sat-urday night and returning the following Saturday morning. We left Saturday, April 26, on the *Cunard Countess*.

Our first stop was Saint Barthelemy followed by Saint Mar-tin. It was a delightful treat on Tuesday to visit Guadeloupe and be met by missionaries Keith and Molly Lancaster. This was wonderful. We not only got a tour of all the beautiful scenery but also got to see the missions work going on there. We were enjoying a picnic in a beautiful park when Eva stepped on a rock, causing her to fall. She broke her ankle in two places. We put her on a flight back to Puerto Rico, and I finished the cruise to fulfill our commitment. The next stop was St. Lucia, where I met missionaries Jon and LaHoma Sin-gleton. In Antigua I met missionaries Donnie and Dimples Bond. On Friday we stopped at St. Thomas, and what a shop-ping tour! I just knew no one would leave those lovely shops to come back to the ship for arts and crafts. I was surprised when seven showed up for the last class. Meeting the other missionaries, enjoying the fellowship with those in my arts and crafts class, the beautiful scenery, and wonderful food all made that cruise so special—another very special fringe bene-fit God had provided along the way.

Seeing so much of God's handiwork was a real treat. The water was beautiful, with only one really rough day. That was my first experience with being seasick. A very kind man shared with me some patches to be worn behind the ear. After a short nap I was up and feeling fine. The people on the ship were delightful. Though I did not participate in many of their activities, they understood and seemed to respect my abstinence of drinking, gambling, etc., because of my faith in God. It really was a once-in-a-lifetime opportunity for me. I took advantage of it and saw everything I possibly could. God really does have a beautiful world.

At every assignment, the FMB always had an auditor to check the books. Every penny is thoroughly accounted for. This has always made me proud of our Southern Baptist Convention. We were delighted to have Don Hart from Venezuela and Frank Johnson from Guatemala to come for our audit. It was a joy to have them in my home for meals, take them shopping, and take them to church. We saw a lot of San Juan while they were there. Frank spoke to our Baptist Women group. It was an excellent opportunity to have a foreign missionary speak. While they were there, I got reports from the field, checked them, balanced them, entered them in the computer, and prepared the final reports for the Richmond, Virginia, office. Only God could have made that possible. Every time I reached the end of my rope, He always took over. I thanked Him every day for His faithfulness and for all those faithful rope holders back home. They had as much responsibility for these experiences as I did. They were on one end of the rope and I was on the other!

Holidays are always very special to those away from home, even though their loved ones are far away. Mother's Day could have been a rough day for me; however, my family and friends did all they could to make it special. I received lovely cards and greetings, a phone call from my children, and a special call from A. L. and Myra Courtney. They were all anxious to know what I was doing for lunch on Mother's Day.

Eight lovely young people who were away from their moms invited me to eat with them. I offered to make a cake, but they declined. They just wanted me to be their mom for the day. It was a special lunch. Earlier that morning the auditors had each given me a box of candy. It seemed that God gave me a family everywhere He sent me.

Sunday, June 29, 1986, Calvary Baptist Church held an open house in honor of Bill and Marjorie Graves. It was a glorious occasion. Bill had spent many years in the Caribbean and was loved by all. They would be sorely missed, but we knew them well enough to know they would be about our heavenly Father's business no matter where they went.

Another dear couple who came to mean a lot to me was James and Sheila Wang. They worked with the Chinese congregation. While I was there, they were appointed by the FMB to be missionaries to the Chinese congregation in the Dominican Republic. Since that time they have done missions work with the Chinese all over the Caribbean.

As the time of the Graveses' retirement grew nearer, we were delighted to learn that Ron Wilson had been appointed to serve in Bill's place. When Ron called to make the arrangements, he asked to spend some time with me. I was thrilled because Ron, Janice, and the children were like family to me.

It was a very busy week. We celebrated Marjorie Graves's birthday with a party, a *bienvenido* (welcome) for the Days who had just returned from furlough, and a *despediza* (farewell) for the Donehoos. I was to move out of the Fred and Janice's apartment and into Wilson and Martha's. Ron Wilson came early one morning to load my suitcases, groceries, and other belongings. Although Ron had a million other things to take care of, he was the one person who was never too busy for anyone else. I am so glad that God let me know him! I had enjoyed living in Fred and Janice's apartment. I especially enjoyed their library. Everywhere I stayed I enjoyed reading the books in the missionaries' homes. It was always a time of discovery. My favorite in the Days' library was a three-volume set by Charles H. Spurgeon, *The Treasury of David*. I could sit for hours in the glory and praise of God as expressed in the Psalms. As soon as I returned home I bought a set of these for myself and my pastor. Now that Fred, Janice, and Mandy Day had returned, I could get acquainted with them personally. The more I knew them, the more I loved them.

Sometimes our homes were like Grand Central Station. Most of the Caribbean missionaries came to Puerto Rico for their vacation or for medical attention. This was a wonderful opportunity for me to get to know many missionaries I had only read about. I loved cooking for them. It was not unusual to have 10 or 12 of them for dinner, but the same menu was often served because each group was different. I never served one who didn't like southern cooking.

One very special treat came when Jim and Anna Laney came from Pell City, Alabama, for a few days. They were there for a cruise, but spent time with me before and after the cruise. It was a rare time with special friends.

During my stay in Puerto Rico I made many wonderful, new friends. Win and Ann Belue and I became very close friends. They were so dear to include me in so many of their activities. Win worked for the Federal Aeronautics Administration. Ann decided she wanted to go to St. Thomas to do some shopping and invited me along. We flew over on a sea-plane, landing in the water near the shore. The pilot put the wheels down and drove the plane right up a ramp and onto a landing spot in the middle of town. The entire day was as exciting as the ride had been. We did some sight-seeing, enjoyed the foods, walked, and shopped.

My weakness has always been tablecloths. I wore out my credit cards that day. All the missionaries knew I would come back with at least one new tablecloth. When I learned my farm was going to sell, they had all laughed about how many table-cloths that money would buy. The day was very special. It was something different just when I needed it. God knew just what I needed and when I needed it. He always supplied abundantly. I have wished so many times that all the wonderful things that happened to me could happen to those at home who were so faithfully holding those ropes.

Ron and Janice Wilson had arrived in Puerto Rico early so they could get the children into school. The guest apartment was full and so was everyone's home, so they had to stay in a hotel. The weekend they went to the Dominican Republic to pack their belongings for shipping, I kept their four children at my apartment. We had a lovely time. At the breakfast table that Sunday morning, John, 5, said, "Aunt Eunice, these are the best homemade eggs I ever ate!"

We all laughed as I asked, "Darling, what makes them homemade?"

He replied, "They are cooked at home!"

It dawned on me that these children had been living in a hotel for ten days. They had been eating in restaurants until even homemade eggs were appreciated. Ron Jr., 15, and Anna, 13, took excellent care of Timothy, 7, and little John. Even in church it was a delight to sit with them. Remember at every opportunity to pray for our missionaries' kids (MKs) and their parents. You never know what their needs might be at any particular moment. Only God can supply their every need!

I went to the missions field to relieve the missionaries of any task I could. The more acquainted a wife becomes with her husband's work, the better helpmate she can be. I wanted to do my part. I told Fred and Janice Day that if they could make some of the missions trips together, I would be glad to have their daughter, Amanda, stay with me. It was one small way I could further their ministry.

The day I turned 66 God once again proved His sufficiency to me. I found myself away from home, doing a job I was not trained for, and accomplishing everything that was needed! God is still in the business of taking loaves and fishes and blessing them to make them sufficient. Someone once said, "He does not always call the qualified, but He qualifies those He calls." I heartily agree.

I received many precious cards, gifts, and letters from home as well as from those in Puerto Rico. David and Laura Silva, a dear young couple, married only one month, invited me to their home after prayer meeting to enjoy a delicious cherry cake. Laura had decorated it with a heart in the center. She worried that her first attempt at baking would not be good. Anything made with that much tender loving care had to be special. David and Laura were both in the new members class I had taught. They were so gracious to me. One Saturday they took me on a picnic to El Morro, one of the most popular sites in Puerto Rico. God knew I needed grandchildren, so He sent David and Laura Silva.

After teaching the new members class, I was asked to teach a youth Sunday School class. I thoroughly enjoyed them. David and Laura helped me with the class; and when I left Puerto Rico, they agreed to teach the youth class.

One of my nicest birthday treats was an invitation from Win and Ann Belue to visit Phosphorus Bay with them. We were to spend the night. I had not seen any of the island since coming to Puerto Rico, so they made this trip around the whole island. On the south side of the island, the car's radiator hose burst. Water came up all over the windshield. Win was afraid that if he stopped the car, it would not start again; so we continued up the mountain. Just over the top, when we were expecting to try and coast down, we spotted a wrecker coming up the other side. Win flagged him down. The driver was so nice that we were all sure God had put this special person there just for us. He spoke English and invited Ann and me to ride in the air-conditioned cab with him. He towed the car to Ponce, the second largest city of the island.

The man took us to an auto parts store, got the hose, and put it on. Then he saw that we also had trouble with the water pump. He took us to his neighborhood and introduced us to the repairman's wife. She contacted her husband for us. We were detained about four hours, but that family treated us like royalty. They had spent some years in New York and spoke beautiful English. We were served lemonade and given a tour of their place. They did not attend church, but they let us witness to them. We praised the Lord for His goodness. It was delightful to get to know a different side of Puerto Rico and its people.

We went on to Phosphorus Bay and registered at an old-fashioned hotel, ate, and went down to the bay for a boat ride. I thought the fish were glowing, but it was the water! There was a beautiful moon, and the attendants brought buckets of water from the bay and poured it on the floor of the boat. It looked like he was pouring out electricity. Then they turned on the lights around the bottom of the boat so we could see the bottom of the bay. It was a very special boat ride.

We spent the night there; and the next morning took the long way around the island, enjoying the fellowship as much as the scenery. I thanked God that He had finally let me see the rest of the island. God had given me special friends everywhere I had gone, and I praised Him for them.

Ron and Janice Wilson were invited to speak at a college retreat, a first for Puerto Rico, and they invited me to go along. It was held on the southern coast of Puerto Rico. All the meetings were in Spanish, with 110 young people attending. The leaders were thrilled with the response. The Wilsons' two youngest boys, Timothy and John, and I played on the beach most of the day. We had so much fun gathering shells and playing ball. The boys were so excited to be outside. They lived in a 15th-floor apartment and never got to play outside unless it was at school. Again you can see why MKs need your prayers. You may never know their specific needs, but you have a tremendous responsibility of intercession.

My departure date had been set before Wilson and Martha Donehoo left on furlough. Wilson had decided that since there was so little activity in the treasurer's office during the holidays, I should plan to be home for Christmas. They would be returning January 1, 1987, and I wanted to be out of their apartment before then. As the holidays neared, plans were made for me to leave on December 16, 1986. Ron and Janice helped me pack and took me to the airport. Once again I was leaving a part of my heart with the precious people I had grown to love. I thanked God for giving me a year in Puerto Rico!

14

God's Plan and Provision for Me

*"Now unto him that is able to keep you from falling, and to
present you faultless before the presence of his glory with exceeding joy, to the only wise God our Saviour, be glory and
majesty, dominion and power, both now and ever. Amen"*
(Jude 24–25).

Furlough time again! I arrived home from Puerto Rico on December 16, 1986. The precious apartment furnished for me by
my home church was a fairyland. It was beautifully decorated
with a live Christmas tree. A wonderful fruit tray and Christmas cookies graced the table. Homemade and canned foods
filled the cabinets, refrigerator, and freezer. It was so very special to spend my first night home in my own little apartment.

God really amazes me at how He puts all things together.
On Christmas Eve my brother, Richard, called and asked what
arrangements I had for a car. I had only rented one for
Wednesday through Friday to get me through the holidays.

Richard said, "That's fine because God has answered your
prayers, but it cannot be delivered until Friday!"

A dear friend, Pete Little, brought me his car on Friday. He
was the same dear one who had sent me the giant jar of peanut
butter while I was in Tanzania.

After completing my assignment in Puerto Rico, the Volunteers in Missions Department of the Foreign Mission Board
(FMB) had mentioned another assignment in Africa. I was

prepared to leave on March 13, 1987, for Nairobi, Kenya, but this assignment did not work out. I am a true believer that absolutely nothing just happens in my life. I accepted this as planned by the precious hand of God.

My church had begun a new Masterlife class in January and I enrolled in it. I knew that even if I did not get to finish it, the things I did learn would be of value.

Most of my time at home was filled with sharing at different churches about my wonderful experiences with God's leading. Some of the churches had me come each time I returned on furlough. Several had named a missions group after me. This had a profound, humbling effect on my life. I did not feel worthy of such an honor. Many remarks were made of my faith and courage, but my answer was always, "No, but I have a wonderful God!"

Some of my Sundays began at 5:30 A.M. with an early morning engagement at a Brotherhood breakfast. Speaking at Sunday School and again at the 11:00 A.M. worship service rounded out my morning. Lunch with a pastor, WMU friends or others, and then on for a 2:00 P.M. meeting, evening worship service, then meetings with youth or others afterward, usually put me in bed around 11:00 P.M. God provided strength each day and a needed message for each hour.

I had many opportunities to speak to civic groups, company banquets, and much more. Anxiety would sometimes creep into my heart. The days were flying by so fast and I so wanted another assignment. In June 1987 I called the FMB and asked about Ethiopia's request for an accountant. Ron Boswell said the request was for a couple, but he agreed to see if they would accept a single person. Ethiopia agreed but wanted someone with a degree in accounting. College degrees were required for a visa, but the FMB decided to try to get me in on my experience. Another call questioned whether I had ever worked with large dollar figures. I had worked almost 20 years for Steel City Construction Company. They had a volume upward of $10 million. I was responsible for the accounting and also the supervision of office personnel. Finally satisfied of my qualifications, they agreed to start proceedings for my visa.

On Sunday, August 2, 1987, I received a call from Ann Smith, a nurse who had served in Ethiopia. Ethiopian missionaries Lynn and Suzanne Groce would be speaking at her church in Bessemer, Alabama, that night. She invited me to come and hear them. I was delighted and excited. I had so many questions! While visiting with Lynn and Suzanne, Lynn commented that it would take a miracle to get me into Ethiopia because I had no degree. Further, only a super miracle would get me there in less than six months. I said when God worked it out and opened the door, I would be ready.

My family and friends were concerned about my possibly going to Ethiopia. It was a communist country and would be very different. As I meditated on 2 Chronicles 16:9, my Masterlife Scripture verse, I read, "For the eyes of the Lord run to and fro throughout the whole earth, to shew himself strong in the behalf of them whose heart is perfect toward him." My heart was not perfect, but I felt there was nothing between my soul and my Savior. I really needed to know His will for this assignment. While looking at this verse, I saw the word *Ethiopia* in the previous verse. It said, "Were not the Ethiopians and the Lubims a huge host, with very many chariots and horsemen? yet, because thou didst rely on the Lord, He delivered them into thine hand." If my heavenly Father had been there in the flesh, He could not have made it any plainer! Never again did I worry about going to a communist country. As I shared this with my family, it was simply, "I must go." It was not necessary that I return home, but it was very necessary that I go!

On Tuesday, August 4, a horrible helicopter crash in Addis Ababa, Ethiopia, killed the treasurer of the Baptist Mission of Ethiopia, Troy Waldron, and the pilot of the Helimission. This tragedy broke hearts throughout the world, and many prayers were offered on behalf of Troy's family and the Baptist Mission of Ethiopia.

The Ethiopia Mission needed someone quickly who could manage the accounting. On August 12, Barbara Wesley called from the FMB and asked if I could leave for Ethiopia on September 2. Super miracle! I had a wedding in my family on

September 5 and was to graduate from Masterlife on September 6. I asked if I could leave on September 7. The FMB was trying to get me a business visa.

On September 1, I received a call saying that my visa had been granted. Praise my wonderful Lord! Rosie Bedsole wrote asking me to bring materials to teach a high school English class. I had not studied English since 1937, exactly 50 years ago. God had never failed me, and I could not afford to worry about it. I ordered the books and made arrangements to have them mailed to Ethiopia as soon as possible.

My church gave me a special send-off. One Sunday School class began planning a supper and another class wanted to help, and then another. It was a very special time. I was presented with a money tree by all the classes. My pastor and his wife gave me a *Thompson Chain Study Bible.* This Bible became a tremendous help in planning Sunday School lessons and Bible studies for the 12th-grade English class. I was scheduled to leave on Wednesday, September 9, 1987.

I was delighted to have my friend Mary Nell Miner help me pack. Another dear friend, Barbara Joiner, came by for a visit. We had recently studied some of her writings on spiritual gifts in Masterlife. She wanted to crawl into one of my boxes and go with me. Rosie Bedsole was one of her dearest friends and she ached to go and visit. My granddaughter, Lexie Perryman, also helped me pack. She stuffed each little soft spot or corner with candy. As we packed, Lexie said, "Grandmother, I am so proud of you. Everyone should have a jet-set grandmother." I laughed so hard! Who would ever think of me as part of the jet set?

I left on September 9, 1987, and spent my 67th birthday in Rome, Italy. My parting prayer requests were:

1. That all my luggage and I would arrive safely and together. It was a big request, but we have a big God!
2. That God would give me the good health necessary for whatever He had planned.
3. That God would equip me with knowledge for the job, wisdom to meet every opportunity with a positive witness, even under heavy restrictions, and the courage that would be necessary.

God answered each of my requests. It never ceased to amaze me that God had chosen me for such a tremendous responsibility. I could have fallen flat on my face. No one has been so unqualified. God, in His marvelous sufficiency, had worked it all together and brought victory. I praised Him every step of the way. To be called to serve the King of kings and Lord of lords, was the greatest opportunity I could ever ask for or even imagine.

During the flight from Rome to Addis Ababa, I met a man going to Ethiopia to work as a doctor. He would be relieving another doctor who was returning home to raise his financial support. They were not Southern Baptists and their denomination did not support its missionaries as the Baptists do. I was proud of our Southern Baptist system. He was a delightful young man and I wish I had gotten his name. He was very helpful to me as we went through customs. I had several heavy pieces of luggage to claim. He gathered them all up and placed them on the counter for me.

While we were waiting in line, a very distinguished Oriental man held out his hand with *Eunice Perryman* written on his palm. He asked if I was Eunice Perryman. I nodded that I was. Jerry Bedsole was outside waiting for me, but was not allowed in customs. This young man had arrived on the same flight and was allowed back inside customs. Jerry had asked him to come in and assist me. God was taking such good care of me. The young doctor left me in capable hands and went to collect his own luggage. I learned later that my second angel was also a doctor. He would be attending the same church I would.

15

Jesus' Commission— Go and Teach

"Fear thou not; for I am with thee: be not dismayed; for I am thy God: I will strengthen thee; yea, I will help thee; yea, I will uphold thee with the right hand of my righteousness"
(Isa. 41:10).

My first few weeks in Addis Ababa, Ethiopia, were very busy. Frank Sisson, another volunteer, had been doing the necessary bookkeeping since Troy Waldron's death. He graciously explained their system and I went right to work.

My orientation to the country and language came second to the accounting. The usual cultural shock of living in a foreign country was more difficult this time. The lifestyle and the system for buying groceries were quite different. The mail also arrived later and took longer, sometimes as much as three weeks. The missionaries and other volunteers were very helpful and eased this transitional period tremendously. The highlight of my week was our Wednesday night prayer meeting.

When I arrived in Addis Ababa there was only one career missionary couple, Jerry and Rosie Bedsole, and about ten volunteers. Rosie told me there were more than 190 applications for the English classes. There would be two or three 12th-grade classes. I was asked to teach all of those. This was a new experience for me. The only classes I had ever taught were Bible classes and office procedures. I chose to use the Gospel of John as my textbook and thanked the Lord for having just completed the Masterlife course. This helped me to outline the lessons.

One day each week was set aside for going to the market. I did not have a vehicle and we lived about ten miles from town. We all loaded into the Bedsoles' van and went to the markets together. There was a vegetable market, full of fruits and vegetables. The meat market did not have much variety. It usually had pork loins, sometimes chicken, and occasionally bacon or beef. Several places sold eggs and yogurt; one had peanut butter. There were also several stores for staples such as flour, rice, jellies, and jams. One such store had a large drum of syrup. I wanted to purchase one kilo of syrup but had no container to put it in. The store owner went next door to a liquor store and came back with an empty bottle. He weighed the bottle and then balanced the scales with something else of the same weight. Then he placed a kilo of canned goods on the opposite scale and poured the syrup into the bottle until the scales balanced. I took my syrup home in a liquor bottle. I took a lot of teasing from friends who were served syrup in my home. The bottle was a great conversation piece.

There was also a government grocery store. It contained imported items such as shortening, canned milk, sugar, and toilet tissue; but everything was very expensive. I was delighted to find these items available, no matter what the cost. My first shopping trip there totaled $144 in US currency. The ratio of Ethiopian *birr* to the American dollar was 2.032 *birr* to 1 US dollar.

I was careful to follow all the instructions of bleaching all fruits and vegetables and boiling my water, but I still came down with the dreaded African disease of diarrhea and vomiting. My antacid was not helping, so Jerry Bedsole gave me a capsule large enough to choke a horse! It did help, though, but only temporarily. I continued to have spells of this disease off and on for several months. Our volunteer doctor, Ron Halbrooks, came into Addis Ababa and gave me medicine which finally stopped the disease. I was able to return to work full-time.

Before Troy Waldron's death, the Mission had made a down payment on a new helicopter. The Mission had been hiring Helimission to furnish a helicopter and pilot. The day our new helicopter was to make its maiden voyage we all went to the airport. We were so excited, we formed a circle around it and committed it to the Lord, praying for safety and thanking God for all the offerings that made it possible. We prayed it would always be used to magnify the name of Jesus Christ.

Many of our clinics and feeding stations were located in mountainous areas which were only accessible by air or hiking. Trips that took seven hours by truck were made in only two hours using the helicopter. I was invited to go along on the maiden voyage but found an excuse. I needed some time to think this over. I asked Jerry if the pilot would please remember that I was elderly and might have a weak heart and could not take any acrobatics. I was assured that the pilot does only what he is told. I knew I didn't stand a chance.

One lovely Saturday night a dear Ethiopian woman who worked at the Mission office, Meseret Mamo, invited all of us to her home for supper. She and her family served an Ethiopian meal, *injera bo wat,* and all the trimmings. It was delicious. This was my first experience with any of the Ethiopian dishes. *Injera,* a bread cooked in something similar to a large wok, was fried like a large pancake or pizza crust. It was then rolled into large rolls and cut into two-inch pieces. This bread was used to pick up meat, vegetables, and gravy. After the meal, the women were taken to the back room for a coffee ceremony. The coffee was ground and put in a pot with a little ball on the top. When the ball began jumping up and down, the coffee was ready. None of the men were allowed to see this ceremony. It was a delight. We had a wonderful time visiting with Meseret's family. There was so much laughter as she taught me how to eat the *injera.* It was delicious! Every time I opened my mouth, someone snapped a picture, threatening to send pictures to my home church and the Foreign Mission Board (FMB). No one has ever enjoyed life more than I have.

The English classes were fantastic. I was not a great teacher, but my heavenly Father took my loaves and fishes and blessed them and multiplied them, making them sufficient. We enrolled 52 12th-grade students. I had one class on Wednesdays and one on Fridays. Following one Friday class I found seven young men waiting in the hall. They said it took two hours to get there and they could not get there in time for my 3:00 P.M. class. I had them take a seat while I went to find Jerry.

Jerry and Rosie were in the office when I came in to ask for advice. I will never forget Jerry's answer. He said, "Eunice, priority number one, 'Go and teach.' Supply the answer to their spiritual needs." I told him I was worried the auditors might need me because of the ongoing audit.

Dan Whorton, an auditor from Richmond, Virginia, repeated Jerry's words. "Go and teach. Priority number one."

Matthew 28:19–20 has never meant the same to me since that day. Jesus used the word *teach* twice in that Great Commission, doubling its emphasis. I returned to my classroom and taught the same John 3 lesson I had taught earlier.

One prayer request I asked for from friends and family at home was to pray for me at 6:00 A.M. on Wednesdays and Fridays. I was nine hours ahead of Alabama time, and those were the hours I taught my class. What a great risk taker God was! So many others could have done a much better job than I could. My inability made me rely totally on my heavenly Father. He did a super job! God had many mountains for me to climb and only through the prayers of others did I make it.

Jewell Waldron had some work in progress when her husband, Troy, was killed on August 4, 1987. She chose to stay and complete it. She had two sons, Nicholas and Timothy, and was two months pregnant with their third child. As her stay in Ethiopia came to a close, she moved into the guest house and began to dispose of her groceries, furniture, etc. I tried to help as much as possible. Every morning I left baked biscuits on their dining room table. The first morning I left them, Nicholas ran in to wake his mother saying, "Mother, the biscuit fairy has been here!" When the children remarked that they were going to the US for forever, it touched everyone in our Mission family. Bob Walls went along on the trip back to the States with Jewell to help her with the boys. We missed them.

16

Yokefellows with God

"Come unto me, all ye that labour and are heavy laden, and I will give you rest. Take my yoke upon you, and learn of me; for I am meek and lowly in heart: and ye shall find rest unto your souls. For my yoke is easy, and my burden is light"
(Matt. 11:28–30).

Some of the most precious volunteers, journeymen, career missionaries, and special assignment personnel I have met were in Ethiopia. Jennie Robeson (now married to Michael Houser), a lovely journeyman and nurse, was one of the dearest people I met. She was stationed up-country on one of the highlands, Meranya, and only came down to Addis Ababa if required. All of the up-country personnel were required to come down to Addis Ababa every six weeks for rest and relaxation. When Jennie came down, she stayed in the guest house, and I adopted her as my own.

Kitty Byrd, another nurse from up-country, was also a delight. Kitty had a clinic and feeding station in Gundo Muskel. While I was in Ethiopia, a meningitis epidemic broke out. Kitty set up an isolation tent for those patients and scheduled personnel to care for them around the clock. Out of 50 meningitis patients she cared for, only 7 died. They died because they waited too long before coming for treatment. During the epidemic the US embassy ordered enough vaccine for all the US personnel. Ed Mason had all personnel up-country brought into Addis Ababa for their vaccinations. We really appreciated our representatives during times like that. They had our best welfare as a top priority.

Special assignment person, Michael Houser, also became dear to me. Michael, a veterinarian did an excellent job in assisting Jerry in Addis Ababa and holding weekly animal clinics up-country. He loved to eat and I loved to cook, so I adopted him immediately. He would sometimes come home from the office with me. We would eat, sit, and talk for hours. He became very special to me.

Another special assignment couple, Bob and Yvonne Walls, worked with the hunger relief program. They were stationed in Alem Ketema but were often in Addis Ababa. They would always eat with me during these visits. Both were always willing to help in any way. Wherever they went, they were a joy.

Also stationed in Alem Ketema were newlyweds Ron Halbrooks and his wife, Mary. Ron, a physician, visited all the up-country clinics, coordinating the medical work. He did an outstanding job. In the ten years I was out of the US, Ron was the only doctor I ever went to for medical attention. Mary had previously taught at Bingham Academy in Addis Ababa. She was the substitute teacher for my English class. Both Ron and Mary were very dear.

Don and Janet Pittman were stationed in Meranya. They had a tree farm, chicken farm, and two oxen for breeding purposes. They also conducted Bible studies and feeding stations. I was delighted to have them eat with me when they came into Addis Ababa. Sometimes they took me out to dinner. I never was able to get my biscuits light and fluffy while there; but Don insisted that I just needed more practice, and heartily volunteered to be my guinea pig. They were a delightful ray of sunshine and a very special witness for the Lord.

One of our greatest days at the Baptist Mission was the day Ed and Vi Mason, a special assignment couple, returned from furlough. They had already served five or six terms directing the hunger relief program. The Ethiopians were also thrilled to have them back. The government offices honored Ed and Vi before they left with a special banquet. Ed's incredible ability to make everyone feel special gave him a very dear place in many hearts. He had an excellent rapport with government officials in Ethiopia. Ed was a lawyer and had also served as president of the Florida Baptist Convention. Ed's efforts through the Baptist Mission were instrumental in establishing a radio system providing contact with all missionaries in the up-country stations.

Vi was a very gracious hostess. Her concern for others endeared her to everyone, including the nationals. It would be impossible to list all their special attributes. They were truly loved by all. Ed and Vi were furnished with a vehicle and never made a trip anywhere without asking if anything was needed or if someone else wanted to go along. We all thanked God for Ed and Vi.

Career missionaries Paul and Hannah Gay arrived in Addis Ababa shortly after I did. Paul was appointed by the Foreign Mission Board (FMB) to serve as an accountant. Hannah was a doctor and would be working to meet the medical needs. They were required to attend language school their first year in Ethiopia. I hoped that I could remain until they completed the school in August 1988.

On December 8, 1987, career missionaries Jeff and Margie Pearson, and son, Christopher, arrived. Jeff was a water engineer and Margie was a nurse. Of course, they also had a year of language school, but they were delightful next-door neighbors. While they were in language school, they hired a lovely Ethiopian woman to help with the housework and take care of Christopher. Christopher would hear Amharic all day and English at night. As he grew older and began putting words together, he had trouble distinguishing between his aunts and uncles. Missionaries' kids (MKs) call all adults in the Mission by these titles. I ended up being called Uncle Nunis. It didn't matter what he called me, just so he called me!

The main event each week was prayer meeting. Friends of other faiths joined us. We shared our joys and sorrows, problems and prayer requests. The Baptist Mission of Ethiopia is a huge operation and absolutely must be founded on prayer. It was wonderful to see how God worked out every problem.

I was in Ethiopia on a 30-day business visa, applying for an extension each month. I never knew when I would have to leave. Knowing it was in God's hands gave me total peace about the situation. Each month Zamichael went for my visa extension and upon his return, I asked, "Do I buy groceries or an airline ticket?" Each month he grinned and I knew the answer; I had gotten another 30 days.

I had been in Ethiopia about five months and did not know if the immigration department would give me a new business visa. It was shared at our prayer meeting that Zamichael had been able to get me a new business visa. After a loud "Yeah!" a very special prayer of thanks was given to God. I had been so sick so much of the time, I was ready to accept whatever God did. He worked out His will and I thanked Him.

17

The Feeding Program

"Inasmuch as ye have done it unto one of the least of these my brethren, ye have done it unto me" (Matt. 25:40).

The week after Christmas, Jerry said there would be an extra seat on the helicopter and he wanted me to go up-country. I was so excited. How I wished everyone back home could have gone with me. This was my first flight in a helicopter. Grant Louden, our pilot, was delightful. He pointed out all the sights from the air.

Our first stop was in Alem Ketema where Ron and Mary Halbrooks lived. After Jerry checked the feeding supplies and met with our team leaders, we went on to Meranya. Don and Janet Pittman, Jennie Robeson, and Keith Riddle lived there. Keith was away from home that day. We had lunch in Meranya while Grant shuttled gravel to two water projects under construction. He invited me to go along, but my stomach was a little upset from all the ups and downs, so I declined.

The highlands were very high, some 10,000 feet above sea level. At some points the earth would drop 5,000 feet straight down. As we flew sometimes only 3 or 4 feet from the ground, we would suddenly fly out over a gorge or canyon dropping 5,000 to 10,000 feet below us. My stomach did somersaults, and I did a lot of praying that day.

Every station had a group of team leaders made up of Christian Ethiopians who had completed the Masterlife program. They had been hired to administer the feeding programs, clinics, water development projects, agricultural projects, and also to help in witnessing.

While Jerry met with the team leaders, Janet and I walked into town. There was a market, but it had little to sell. We were the big attraction. Such a mob gathered around us that it was difficult to move, so we headed back to the Baptist compound. The mob followed us all the way, but even the little children holding my hand knew they could not come inside the gates. The gates were guarded to protect our premises.

Don Pittman showed us the work he was doing and where the veterinary clinics were held. Jennie showed us her clinic and treated some patients while we were there. Many times the Baptist Mission clinics had medicines that were not available elsewhere only because Southern Baptists were so faithful to provide them.

We returned to Alem Ketema and picked up Kitty Byrd and all her refrigerated items we had brought from Addis Ababa. We took her to Gundo Muskel where she held her clinics and feeding station. Everywhere we landed Jerry met with team leaders while I took pictures of all the work being done in the area. After leaving Gundo Muskel we went to Rema where we had a feeding station and team members, but no missionaries. After Jerry met with the team members, we returned to Alem Ketema where we would spend the night.

At Jerry's suggestion Grant flew low in many areas so I could see the crocodiles, monkeys, baboons, and deer families (buck, doe, and baby). They called it the scenic route. At one point the door nearest me came open! I realized I had not closed it very well. It looked like we were 10,000 feet high! Grant quickly said, "Don't panic, Eunice, I will fix it."

I answered, "I am not going to panic. I am fastened in so tightly with all these belts, I could not possibly fall out!"

He reached across me and pulled the door closed. Grant never knew how much my stomach was rolling and tumbling! It was a once-in-a-lifetime experience. *Thank You, Lord!*

During one of our flights, Jerry pointed out a village on the horizon. He said that not one denomination had ever been into that area with the gospel. He hoped that one day we could go there. Many times I have prayed that God will let our missionaries get into that particular area and share His love.

When we arrived in Alem Ketema, we heated the beef stew I had brought with us. After a hot meal, we were ready for bed. The next morning we went to Behera where our agricultural department has a small country home where materials are stored. Don Pittman and two workers were threshing wheat with the two oxen. He had an excellent tree farm, chickens, sheep, and was doing it all with the barest of necessities. Jerry met with the state agricultural officials and Grant caught up on some paperwork. I laid down and rested.

Our next stop was Mahal Meda. I saw where the Bedsoles, Groces, and Sam and Ginny Cannata had lived before the Communist takeover in 1974. They had not been able to return since the overthrow of Haile Selassie's regime. The next stop was Rabel where Jerry and Grant ate *injera bo wot* with the team members. My stomach was still upset; so I just ate a few cookies, bread, and water. The nationals understood. We flew on to Shila Faf where Jerry met with another team while I went into their chapel for some prayer and quiet time. The chapel was built out of grain sacks. The cushions were made of straw and the walls were made from grain sacks framed with poles.

We arrived back in Addis Ababa about 6:00 P.M. After a hot bath, I was ready for bed. At 12:20 A.M. I awoke and ran to the bathroom. There I was sitting on the commode and vomiting into the bathtub. My first thought was, *Now, Lord, how can I be thankful for these circumstances?*

God answered, *Be thankful it did not happen last night where the outhouses were 200 feet from the house and it was so dark!*

I thanked the Lord I was home. After a few days of recuperating, I would not have taken a million dollars for the experiences I had.

For Ed and Vi Mason's anniversary, I invited them to supper. I also invited our precious pastor and his wife, Bark and Carleen Fahnestock. Vi's favorite pie was lemon; Ed's was coconut; Bark's was chocolate. I made one of each and we all had a small slice of each of them. One thing is for sure, we never lacked for food! When it was my turn to host the prayer meeting, I would make three chocolate pies and three coconut pies. Ed Mason named me chief coconut cream pie maker.

Because I lived in the guest house, I hosted the young people who came from up-country. I always felt they would have more fun without an older person along whenever they invited me out for supper. They never seemed to mind having me along. They probably needed a grandmother as much as I needed the grandchildren, so I adopted them all.

Every day at 8:00 A.M. and 5:30 P.M. the men in our Mission would contact all the up-country stations by radio. One morning all the men were to be out of the office, and I was to contact the up-country stations. I said, "Calling all stations. All operators are out, so tune back in at 5:30 P.M. and they will be here for messages. Over and out."

I was surprised that someone answered back! "Well, hello Eunice, how are you?"

Another said, "We surely are glad to know you are going to be around a little longer."

They wanted to hear some more of my southern drawl. I loved them all!

One weekend Ed and Vi Mason, Bob and Yvonne Walls, and I went to the Awash Game Park. After breakfast at my house, we took off for a wonderful time of seeing God's glorious creations and beautiful world. We laughed so much that weekend and all of us felt God's blessings in a wonderfully special way.

In April 1988 Vi Mason and Yvonne Walls and I went to Kenya. I had really needed to get away for awhile, so this was a welcome retreat. We stayed at the Norfolk Hotel in Nairobi. It was fantastically decorated as an old mansion. On Sunday night we boarded a train to Mombasa, a coastal city of the Indian Ocean. Even though we had sleeper cars, I could not sleep. I was afraid I would miss something. It was very dark out, and I was glad when we arrived in Mombasa. The hotel and beach were what I had imagined Hawaii to be like. We rested until Wednesday evening, then boarded the train back to Nairobi, arriving on Thursday morning. A tour car met us at the train to take us the four-hour drive to Maasai Mara Game Park. We saw a lot of Kenya on our way. The hotel there had a lovely buffet. It included eight or ten meats, twice as many different vegetables, and all kinds of salads and desserts.

After the buffet we rested until 4:00 P.M. when our tour to see all the animals began. That evening and all the next day we saw 23 different animals, including lions and crocodiles. We returned to Nairobi on Saturday and attended the English church on Sunday. I received my visa at the US embassy while we were in Nairobi. I was very thankful.

Upon my return I received a request from the Mission of Ethiopia to extend my stay from September 1988 to December 1988. I spent much time in prayer and talked with Jerry about it. I asked if he thought we could get a third business visa. He said no one had ever gotten a second business visa until I did. He said, "God brought you here; and if He wants you to stay, He will make it possible. We really do need you!" I said I would stay until God closed the door, or mid-December, whichever came first.

One of the hardest things I had to do was watch those precious people I loved so much leave Ethiopia and return to the States. I never knew if I would see them again. Don and Janet Pittman and Keith Riddle were to leave in April. All of them had become so dear to me, and I knew I would really feel the loss. I mothered them all during their last week in Ethiopia. Now that they were leaving, who would I practice my biscuits on? They were asked to give their testimonies at prayer meeting before they left. The progress of their agricultural program was interesting, but the most precious thing they shared was the results of their Bible studies. All three had witnessed a miracle as a Muslim priest was led to Christ. We praised Him mightily! This same priest is now leading others to his Lord. May his number be multiplied! Three others had accepted Christ during their last month. God opens doors in other areas, but the main goal of every volunteer is to share Jesus Christ with a lost world. *Thank You, Lord, for letting us see the results of our labor.* It seems that a missions field is constantly coming and going. When we saw them off, we knew they would continue being missionaries wherever they went. *Thank You, Lord, for letting me know them.*

As soon as some missionaries leave, there are others to take their places. One of those was a dear, dear woman, Mary Saunders, a nurse and the wife of Davis Saunders, an FMB administrator. Every year Mary spends at least two months up-country, working in the clinics and teaching Bible studies. She is loved by both missionaries and nationals. She and her husband had served in Africa and spoke Swahili, not Amharic, so Mary needed an interpreter. Her most fluent language was the language of love. For that, she needed no interpreter. She magnified Jesus Christ in every step and word.

I invited her to speak to my Sunday School class and they fell in love with her too. We asked her to share her testimony in prayer meeting that week. After a short bout of the African intestinal disease, she was able to go up-country and begin her ministry again. Many of the team members remembered her from previous years and were excited to have her return.

Agricultural journeyman, George Tupper, came into Addis Ababa that same week. He stayed in the guest house until he received all the necessary orientation, drivers license, etc. He was ready to go up-country, but I worried that he was still exhausted from jet lag. I felt he should stay at least through the weekend and rest. Jerry assured him that Mama Eunice would take good care of him.

The war in the northern part of Ethiopia was taking its toll on all of Ethiopia. Because Southern Baptists have a policy to stay completely out of any political situation, all we could do was pray. My prayer requests to those back home were:

1. Pray for the leaders in Ethiopia who must make the decisions.

2. Pray for the physical strength of the Ethiopians.
3. Pray for believers in Ethiopia who are having a rough time.
4. Pray for the Baptist Mission of Ethiopia to make wise decisions and be God's representatives.

We really lived on those prayers. Much of our feeding program was frozen. Our helicopter was grounded. Through it all, we knew that God was in control.

18

Hands Busy for God

"Wist ye not that I must be about my Father's business"
(Luke 2:49).

Jim Houser, associate to the area director of East Africa, and his wife, Molly, came to Ethiopia to survey all the work being done there. Jerry planned to take them up-country. He asked if I would like to go along since the Housers were friends of mine from Tanzania.

I packed some food for the trip. We got an early start, arriving at our first station in Alem Ketema about 10:30 A.M. Grain was transported by truck to this station then flown by Polish planes to the other feeding stations. The pilot removed some of the sacks of grain and we crawled into the plane and flew over to Gundo Muskel. It was nice to visit with Kitty Byrd and Mary Saunders again. Along with Ron Halbrooks they treated 357 patients in one day at a huge medical clinic. A very large compound encompassed the clinic and feeding area. She took me outside the gates to show me the enormous amount of people waiting for food and medical attention. The whole top of this highland was covered in people!

I worried that it was not possible to see them all in one day. Kitty said that those who were not seen today would stay the night. There was nothing to go home to. They have said to us, "There is no use for us to go home. There is no food there.

Apart from the Baptists, there is no hope for us except to die. We just stay until we receive food." Grain was issued according to the size of the family, but not exceeding 25 pounds of grain per family. This would last them one month.

Much of the grain distributed by our personnel was provided by other relief organizations. Canadian, US, and many European relief organizations brought their grain into the Southern Baptist warehouses. They knew it would be distributed only to those in need. Southern Baptists had ten large trucks solely to deliver the grain to the people. I was so thankful to be a Southern Baptist. It was an honor to be trusted by so many people.

We watched the food program in action that day as grain and milk powders were distributed to about 3,000 people. The doctors and nurses did not stop to prepare a meal for themselves. I was glad I had brought along some food. We cried awhile, watched some more, took some pictures, and cried some more. *Oh, heavenly Father, how much we take for granted in the US. We have so much for so many to have so little.* It seemed that what we were doing was just a drop in the bucket. At least we tried.

Because we had no helicopter, we climbed aboard another Polish plane and returned to Alem Ketema. This time there were no grain sacks to sit on, so we sat right down on the floor of the plane. Getting down was easy enough, but getting back up was another story. Getting in and out of cargo planes was no easy task, but the experience was very special.

The next morning we visited other sites where the same relief program was taking place. Around noon we returned to Alem Ketema and loaded our things onto the truck for the trip back to Addis Ababa. On our way back we discussed the operation taking place. It was really keeping God busy! All of those planes flying, trucks being driven, and people working together could only be put together by God. They were all volunteers. Not one single career missionary was stationed up-country. It was a tremendous undertaking. God is so sufficient! I thank God for letting me see it and also for letting me have a small part in it.

Communist rule had only allowed two churches to remain open—the International Evangelical Church of Addis Ababa and the Ethiopian Orthodox Church. Every Sunday we all left the compound to worship at the International Evangelical Church. It was composed of many different denominations and was conducted in English. At one time there were 78 embassies represented in this church.

Harold Jongeward introduced himself to me shortly after I began attending this church. He taught seventh- and eighth-grade Sunday School. He needed a substitute for six weeks. He had no materials to teach with so I would have to make my own. Of course, I volunteered for the job.

I found out later that Harold Jongeward was the principal of Bingham Academy in Addis Ababa. My first thought was, *How will I ever follow this person?* God is always sufficient, and before that Sunday afternoon has passed, He had led me to the Book of Daniel, giving me lessons those young people could relate to. I did not find out until much later that Rosie Bedsole had given Harold Jongeward my name. She said, "I just told him that the woman over there loves the Lord and loves young people!" I added another job to my responsibilities and was delighted when every one of my students memorized the books of the Bible as we studied them.

Bark Fahnestock, our pastor, and his wife, Carleen, became dear to me. Soon after completing my substitute teaching, I was asked to take a permanent class of ninth- and tenth-graders. I was so delighted. I felt a freedom to teach as the Lord led, preparing my own lessons and typing the Bible verses so that students would have their own copies. Very few people owned a Bible and no one carried them openly on the streets.

During the church services, I would share my Bible with those sitting near me. It was touching to see the way they held that Bible so tenderly and stroked it in reverential awe. Many times I could not read the passages because of the tears in my eyes. Oh, how much we take for granted the freedoms we enjoy. How many Bibles are lying around in homes in America gathering dust from not being used?

In June 1988 our FMB auditor, Dan Whorton, came to Addis Ababa. He brought me a large bag of pecans, a treasure in Africa. Dan stayed in the guest house, and since I was the unofficial hostess, I prepared his meals. He truly enjoyed hot biscuits for breakfast and was so easy to please. He enjoyed everything I cooked. I enjoyed having that time with him and hearing about his work in Richmond, Virginia.

One Sunday I asked Dan to teach my Sunday School class with me. It was a special experience. We had planned a lesson titled, "How to Have a Full and Meaningful Life." I had prepared copies of the lesson so each person would have a copy. We felt God leading that class. I asked for every head to bow and asked for any who had opened their hearts to the Lord to raise their hands. Eight young people accepted Christ! It was so special and evident that the Holy Spirit was present.

Extending an invitation was not customary in Ethiopia. I had not discussed this with the other missionaries beforehand. I just knew God promised in John 15:16 that He ordained me and sent me forth to bear fruit. I am so grateful that Jesus Himself said those words. I had gone through every open door in Ethiopia, and yet, I had not seen any fruit. God is faithful and He keeps His promises. I had finally seen those fruits! I did not hesitate when the Holy Spirit moved me to offer that invitation. I only acted accordingly.

I was delighted that Dan Whorton was a part of that experience. So often we in accounting stay behind the scenes. We do not always have an opportunity to get involved in actual witnessing. Only when I allowed God to use me in areas other than accounting did my blessings rain. I later had three more decisions in my class. Before Dan left he gave me a beautiful leatherbound copy of *My Utmost for His Highest* by Oswald Chambers. I had worn out one copy before coming to Ethiopia and had not brought it with me.

I enjoyed many special times, especially during meals with all the guests. Our conversations sometimes resembled the comedy routine, "Who's on first?"

I would say, "The ribs on this end of the platter are cured."

Mike Houser, our veterinarian, would reply, "Cured from

what? Were they sick? Are you serving us one of my failures again?"

I sometimes laughed until I cried. We always forgot the circumstances, problems, and tensions that tried to dominate our days and just thanked the Lord for each other!

Teaching a high school English class was one of my best fringe benefits. The first half of each lesson was spent on the Gospel of John, and the second half on words, sentence structure, etc. I never realized how hard the English language is to learn as a second language.

I had studied Swahili in Tanzania, Spanish in the Caribbean, and Amharic in Ethiopia. All of these languages have rules that hold true. But the English language has so many exceptions to the rules. I had to learn the rules all over again before I could teach them to my class. This gave me an opportunity to witness.

The students were so precious. Although I never felt free to offer an invitation during class, each student heard the gospel. One assignment was turned in with a note written on it, saying, "I want to accept Christ as my Lord." That one note made all the cost and sickness of this trip worth every bit of it. I thanked the Lord for bringing me to Ethiopia.

Graduation day was so special for me and for the students as well. I baked a chocolate pound cake, cookies, and brought plenty of soft drinks. I wanted the day to be special. Rosie Bedsole came and talked to the students. Ed Mason came and took pictures. My class presented me with a lovely plaque with Ethiopian musical instruments on it. A note attached to the back read, "To: Eurice Perryman—This givt has given to you in the name of my classmates. This is the approval, that you are sincere to us. I would like to thank you for your dedication, love and fellowship. Really I do appreciate it. May God protect you and bless you in a special way."

I may not have taught them everything, but the note could not have been more special to me if it had been written in perfect English. After all, if *give* is spelled with a *v*, then why would *gift* not be spelled with a *v*? The important thing was they knew I loved them.

I presented a Bible to the ten who graduated. They were so excited about having a Bible of their own. Mizan, one of the students who could not be there on graduation day, came later to receive his Bible. He hung his head and very slowly said, "You have no idea how long I have prayed for a whole Bible." All the hours I had labored on those lessons did not equal the joy I felt. I thanked God for letting me teach those precious young people.

19

And Then the Rains Came

"Behold, I will do a new thing; now it shall spring forth; shall ye not know it? I will even make a way in the wilderness, and rivers in the desert" (Isa. 43:19).

After an eight-year drought, God answered all of our prayers. The bottom fell out! The rains started in June 1988 and lasted through September 1988. Even with a full rainy season, the feeding programs would still be needed until the end of the year. The rains were so heavy in some places that the rivers ran over their banks and washed out bridges. This made it difficult to get the seed grain to some of the feeding stations in the up-country. Thankfully, God always takes over when man has done all he can. We just stood back and watched God work it all together and praised Him. Jerry wanted to take me back up-country to show me the difference the rains made, but I never did get to go back.

Our Masterlife materials were eventually translated into Amharic and stencils made for copies. This was like a dream come true. I knew what Masterlife meant to me and I knew what it could do for the Ethiopians. There were 44 in attendance at the Masterlife seminar. Seven Ethiopian women stayed in our guest house. They each lead Bible study groups in their own homes. Each of those groups could be a potential church when churches are permitted again. I prepared goodies for them to enjoy each night while they studied their Masterlife material. It was a sweet time. Carroll Shaw, the Masterlife director of East and South Africa, came to direct the workshop. He was delightful.

Jerry Bedsole was suffering with back problems, but on Thursday, he came in and sat at a back table to see his lifelong dream taking place. He could not bear to miss seeing the students receive their certificates.

One of the women staying with me in the guest house was director of the university fellowship. She asked if she could attend my Sunday School class. I explained that it was only a ninth- and tenth-grade class, but she still wanted to come. The last night of the seminar I made a banana pudding and invited Carroll Shaw and Ed Mason to come over. After a delightful evening of fellowship, this same young woman asked if she might sing a song for us. Meseret interpreted it for us saying the love of God was sweeter than honey. She had written this beautiful song! It was a time such as this that words cannot describe. It made all our efforts and all our translating pay off. I just praised God that He had let—even me—be a part of it!

Mary Saunders had served in the up-country for almost three months. She came through Addis Ababa and spent the weekend with me at the guest house. It was a most memorable time. I had mentioned seeing a lot of devotionals from a book entitled *With Christ in the School of Prayer* by Andrew Murray. I talked about getting a copy when I got back to the States. She had been teaching from the same book up-country! Mary gave me her own copy, with all her precious notes written in the margins. I spent the rest of my time there in Ethiopia (when I had time) studying this book. God knew I needed it. Yes, we do have a great God!

20

The Heartbreak of Missions

"He will not suffer thy foot to be moved: he that keepeth thee will not slumber. Behold, he that keepeth Israel shall neither slumber nor sleep" (Psalm 121:3–4).

I worked at the office from 8:00 A.M. to 5:00 P.M., with an hour for lunch, Monday through Friday, and Saturday from 8:00 A.M. until noon. My main responsibility was to keep the books on three different accounts. When time came for the budgets to be set, I was really busy with budget requests. Finally, we were able to bring it all together. Our largest budgeted account was drought and famine relief. The agriculture project and Mission budgets were also large accounts.

We found that we could get more done after 5:00 P.M. than we did when the office was open. Several nights we worked until 9:00. without the usual interruptions. One particular night I called it a day at 1:00 A.M. I left the men still working. Sunday afternoons were also spent at the office, but it was wonderful knowing I was right where God wanted me to be and having a part in His kingdom's business.

We finally finished the budgets and sent them to the area office in Nairobi. No problems were found in our budgets, and they were soon approved. We knew we could function for another year. How we praised God for Southern Baptists. I am so thankful that I am a Southern Baptist.

During August fighting broke out between the army, police, and nationals. It took place on both sides of our Baptist Mission compound. We were advised to get in our houses and stay there. We heard shooting during a prayer meeting at the home of Paul and Hannah Gay. We received a telephone call telling us no one was to leave the compound. Those who had come in from other areas were advised to stay. Jerry was still not able to get out of bed because of his back. By Sunday we were able to go to church, but we still kept a very low profile.

Later in August we were able to have our annual Mission meeting. John Faulkner and his wife, Anne, came from Nairobi for our meeting. His news was not good. We would have to cut our budgets by 12 percent. He explained that because of a shortage in Cooperative Program and Lottie Moon Christmas Offering for Foreign Missions gifts, all budgets had to be cut. He also stated that at the end of 1988 the medical programs would cease. All special assignment personnel would be phased out of our programs. Many tears were shed during that meeting.

So many things could not be cut, such as schooling for missionaries' children, housing for the missionaries, and office expenses. Items that could be cut, like gasoline for up-country trips into new areas, were cut. In my mind I saw that little village on the horizon, for which there might never be a next year. I knew that they would be unable to go that far next year. If only every Southern Baptist could go just once and see the faces of those so anxious to hear the gospel. People would not find it so easy to cut gifts to these offerings. Rather, we would find ourselves personally sacrificing so could give more.

Jerry and Rosie Bedsole were returning to Birmingham, Alabama, where Evan Zeiger would operate on Jerry's spine. I stayed at the Bedsole home with the boys until they returned to school. Paul Gay took Peter to Bingham Academy where he would board. The Masons took Paul and Phil to the airport where they boarded a plane for Rift Valley Academy in Nairobi, Kenya.

All the time spent on budgets and the worry and stress from the cutbacks had taken its toll on me. I found myself unable to get out of bed for several days. Vi, Kitty, Betty, and Margie doubled my doses of medicine and vitamins and lovingly nursed me back to health. I thanked God for all of them!

On Friday, September 9, 1988, the Masons took me to the Awash Game Park for my birthday. Kitty Byrd was in Addis Ababa for her break and we invited her to go along. It was a delightful trip and we rested much of the time. As we drove along trying to spot as many different animals as we could, we marveled at the scenery. The water was raging in the rivers, spilling over the banks. The falls were terrific. We saw three huge turtles! My 68th birthday was Saturday, September 10. Vi, Ed, and Kitty made it so very special. We returned to Addis Ababa on Sunday.

There was a note from Dan Whorton waiting for me when we returned. It stated there might be an opening for a book-keeper in Hong Kong! *Dear Lord, are you finally going to let me see China?* Things did not work out, and I was to wait a while longer before God moved on this request.

On September 20 my business visa expired. When Za-michael returned from his usual trip he was not smiling. I knew something was wrong. He said the immigration officials said they had given me 12 months and could not give me any more extensions. There were tears on his face. I asked how long I had and he said, "Fifteen days."

Yes, Lord, I can accept no. I again commit it to You.

At the office the next morning Bob and Ed started telling me how sick they had been with chills and fever. I could not imagine what on earth was wrong. They finally explained that it was withdrawal pains. Bob said he could not bear to do without the coconut pies. Ed suggested the Mission send me to Nairobi to apply for a visitor visa so I could turn the books over to Paul Gay. The process began and Vi said she would go with me. Such friends. They were so special.

Later the same day Ed Mason and Jeff Pearson were sitting in my office discussing what was happening when a very distinguished man walked in. He asked, "Eunice, when can you teach me how to study the Bible?" I was shocked.

Any of the missionaries could have taught him, but he asked me. *Lord, why?* When I regained my composure, I said, "How about right now, during lunchtime?" He wanted no interruptions, so we set it up for Monday from 7:00 A.M. until 8:00 A.M. He would come to my apartment where we would not be disturbed. When he learned I would be leaving soon, he asked if he could also come on Saturday and Monday. *Lord, he is a Harvard graduate. How can I teach him? You must really do all of this because I am totally incapable.*

I called home and talked with my pastor, A. L. Courtney. He went into overtime praying for my visa and also for this teaching opportunity. God was in control. I knew there were two things I had to do before I left Ethiopia. I must have the Fahnestocks to my home for a meal and I must complete the sessions with this special student.

Our first session was on Saturday morning. I learned that God had gotten his attention through the death of a loved one. He wanted to know what Baptists believe. He had lots of other questions.

I had the Fahnestocks for supper that night. We had pork roast, gravy, mashed potatoes, green beans, spinach, coleslaw slaw, gelatin salad, papaya, hot biscuits, two coconut pies, and two chocolate pies. The power went off just as we sat down to eat so we enjoyed a candlelight dinner. It was wonderful. Later, five people who were staying in the guest house joined us for dessert. It was a special evening.

My Sunday School class was growing and learning so well, I hated to give it up, but I told the Fahnestocks they would be needing a new teacher. We were studying the first chapter of John.

Monday morning my special student came again. We studied God's Word. Our first lesson was on the Ethiopian treasurer under Queen Candace and his encounter with Philip. The second lesson was on Saul's experience on the Damascus road.

On Tuesday, September 27, Vi and I left for Nairobi. Upon our arrival we went directly to the area director's office and filled out the forms for a visa. Bob and Barbara Hunter had been transferred from Ethiopia to the Nairobi office. Bob said he would process the forms. As I handed him the papers, Barbara asked, "Do you really want to go back?"

I answered, "Please, don't push it. If I receive a visa, I want it to be simply God working it out. Please don't plead one way or the other."

While I waited I sent a telex to the Foreign Mission Board (FMB) expressing my interest in the Hong Kong assignment. The answer was that the request for a bookkeeper had not materialized. Immediately my mind went back to David Livingstone's words, "Lord, send me anywhere, only go with me. Lay any burden on me, only sustain me. Sever any tie except the tie that binds me to Thyself!" I thought there was no way I would receive a visitor visa back to Ethiopia. Once the immigration officials saw that I had been there 12 months, they would not possibly give it to me.

I was wrong. Although we were told it would be Friday before we had an answer, Bob called on Thursday. My visa was ready! *Thank You, Lord!* Before leaving Nairobi I purchased a ticket for my flight home, leaving Addis Ababa on November 4, 1988. That gave me 30 days to work with my special student; dispose of clothes, groceries, etc.; and close out my bookkeeping assignment.

If ever a volunteer had learned to be flexible, I had. My student came diligently every morning. He spoke beautiful English and had a vast knowledge of the Bible. This sometimes brought about arguments. One morning I said, "I do not know all the answers. I do not even know why you asked me to teach you. I have no college and no seminary training. There are others who could answer all your questions. They are so much smarter than I am."

He held up both hands, and answered, "I am sorry. I promised myself I would not be argumentative. As to why I chose you to teach me, I have seen within you a clean heart, and I wanted to learn from it!"

I had not realized he had been watching me. I never questioned his requests again. During the next 30 days I was often awakened at 3:00 A.M. as God gave me direction for the next lesson. We were studying the Book of John and God magnified Himself. It was disappointing that this man did not find that personal surrender God was calling him to. He did admit to being incomplete and to wanting an experience like Saul had. He promised me before I left that if he ever came to know Jesus Christ as I knew Him, he would write and tell me. I have never received that letter, but that special student is still on my prayer list. I had to leave him for the Holy Spirit to nourish and convict. During one of our last classes, Ed Mason interrupted just long enough to give this student a special *Thompson Chain Study Bible,* which he had held very dear. Ed had been led to give it to this student, feeling he needed it more. *Precious Father, I thank You for giving me this opportunity. Now I leave him with You.*

Tuesday, October 11, Jerry and Rosie Bedsole returned from the States. His surgery and recovery had gone well. During lunch that day, I told Jerry about the Hong Kong assignment. He challenged me to claim Psalm 37:4 as my own. "Delight thyself also in the Lord; and he shall give thee the desires of thine heart." I did claim that verse. I talked to the Lord and laid it to rest. I forgot about it, but God did not.

At my last prayer meeting my prayer was for this special student God had given me. My prayer request was that God would give him a special salvation experience. Michael Houser voiced a specific prayer for me. I had come to love all of the Mission family so much. Yes, I would leave a part of my heart there also. The Ethiopian Mission would have a devout prayer partner for as long as I live.

We had held our usual Wednesday prayer meeting on Tuesday night that week because some of our men were going up-country on Wednesday morning. That morning Margie Pearson was sharing some prayer requests with us over the radio and Ed told her we had already had that week's prayer meeting. She radioed back that God only heard prayers on Wednesday nights. We all enjoyed precious times, knowing our heavenly Father hears every prayer. He never slumbers and always has His ear tuned to us.

Vi and Ed gave a dinner in my honor on Wednesday night. Bark and Carleen Fahnestock and Eshetu Giorgis were there too. It was a very dear time of sharing what my experience in Ethiopia had meant to me. I had privately shared with Bark that the next morning would be my last class with my special student. I was at a loss about what to teach. He suggested that I had done all I could and maybe it was time to let God take over. How I appreciated that! We all sat around the table until after 10:00 P.M., just enjoying being together. Ed and Vi gave me a beautiful Ethiopian cross, carved from ivory, on a red velvet plaque. It now hangs in my living room, a memory of a precious couple and a very special time in my life.

The Mission held my farewell party at Costellos', a lovely restaurant. They gave me a lovely Ethiopian dress and a silver waterpot on a chain—the symbol of the water of life. I love them all so very much.

The day before I left I went to the office for a short while. The up-country radioed in and the Meranya Tabernacle Choir sang for me. "We love you, Eunice, Oh yes, we do. We don't love anyone as much as you. When you're not with us, we're blue. Oh, Eunice, we love you."

After I had a good cry and got off the radio, all the women went into Addis Ababa for a meeting of the International Women's Club at the Hilton Hotel. The hotel had a beauty salon there, so I decided to get a shampoo and set. My appearance would be very different from my appearance when I returned from Tanzania! Ed and Eshetu met Vi and me for lunch at the China Bar. It was so special.

I received a call from Nairobi while I was packing. I would not be able to leave on Friday night, but KLM would put me up in a hotel and I could leave on Saturday night.

The morning I left, all of the Ethiopian office workers gathered outside my apartment and at the office for a last farewell. *Lord, how can I get through these times? When I look at these precious people, I know I may never see them in this life again.* I must move forward! God brought me here and now it was time for another phase of my life to begin. This had been one of my most precious assignments.

Vestal and Carol Jean Blakely, whom I had known in Tanzania, met me at the airport in Nairobi and took me to the hotel. God had angels to care for me every step of the way. At the airport on Saturday night they could not find my luggage. Ed Mason had checked it in at Addis Ababa to go all the way to Birmingham and it had been stored in Nairobi. The ticket agent asked if I wanted to go ahead without my luggage. I assured him that I did! The plane was late in arriving and just before it arrived a KLM staff member came to me and told me they had found my luggage and processed it. I had been told I would have to pay extra for excess baggage. I asked him about this and he said it was not necessary. I asked about going through customs. He said, "No, just go on and have a good trip." I actually looked around to see if God was standing there in the flesh! I knew He had to be in control. Ed Mason was not there, so it had to be God. I was only allowed 44 pounds and I had 154 pounds. Not a penny extra had been charged. Also, I had not bothered to lock my luggage, thinking customs would have to inspect it first, so all my luggage traveled unlocked. Absolutely nothing was missing when I opened it.

The plane finally left at 3:30 A.M. for a 9½ hour flight to Amsterdam, then a 2-hour layover, and another 9½ hours of flying to Atlanta. After 2 hours in Atlanta, going through customs, and a 50-minute flight to Birmingham, I was finally home! I had never been so glad to see my family and loved ones who had prayed me safely there and back. I was completely worn out.

I spent most of the next week sleeping. I never realized how much the traveling had taken out of me. Of course, I was growing older, so that was to be expected. I would not have taken the whole world in exchange for these precious experiences. It truly seemed that I had experienced God every day of this trip. My prayers for those left in Ethiopia were:

1. Good health for the work He has called you to do.
2. Wisdom for every decision.
3. Remembrance of His Word for every opportunity.
4. Fruit from all your labors.

21

My Sufficient Savior

*"Now thanks be unto God, which always causeth us to tri-
umph in Christ, and maketh manifest the savour of his knowledge by us in every place" (2 Cor. 2:14).*

Having been sick so often in Ethiopia, my first priority was to
get a physical. I did not appreciate the doctor's first statement
which began, "At your age." I did agree with his advice to get
lots of rest. However, rest would have to wait until the foreign
missions emphasis was over. No one who had ever been involved in mission service overseas could be still during the
fall of the year.

Shortly after the new year, 1989, I was contacted by the
Home Mission Board (HMB) with a request from the Dakota
Southern Baptist Fellowship. They needed a bookkeeper to
help Jan Dixon, a young woman in their office. In February, I
wrote back explaining that because of so much arthritis I
would not be able to function in cold weather and regretfully
turned down this request.

As time went by I began to think it would probably not be
possible for me to take any more long-range assignments. I decided I needed a larger place to live. The garage apartment the
church had given me had been perfect for short stays; but if I
was to be home for long periods of time, I would need a larger
place. I wanted to be able to entertain my family as well as
have missionaries stay during their visits. A friend told me of a

house right in town, but a house and all the maintenance that went with it did not seem like the ideal thing for me. I continued searching for a two- or three-bedroom apartment with a dining room. There was not one to be found in Pell City.

The second time this house was mentioned I listened a little more closely. A very dear minister, George Williams, and his wife, Naomi, had deeded the house, upon their death, to the Baptist Foundation of Alabama. The deed included all the furniture too. Monday morning I spoke with my pastor about the house. He dialed the foundation office in Montgomery and was soon talking with Warren Trussell, president of the foundation. After making the introductions, he handed me the phone. I talked with Warren Trussell in detail. Two days later I was signing the papers for the house and furniture. It had been sitting for one year just as they had left it. George Williams had died while I was in the Caribbean and Naomi had died while I was in Ethiopia.

God worked it all together. My new house was completely furnished. I have a three-bedroom home, one and one-half baths, and a two-car garage. I am only three blocks from the church, grocery store, and drugstore; two blocks from city hall, the courthouse, and the bank; and one block from the library. Yes, only God could have done this!

The request from North Dakota continued to come back to me and I finally consented to go July and August of 1989. Surely there would be no blizzard during those two months. Once again my church assured me they would take care of my little house while I was off to the wild blue yonder. I had been east, south, and now I was headed north.

Jan Dixon was a precious young woman and very anxious to learn more about her bookkeeping job. It was a delight to work with her. The executive director of the Dakota Southern Baptist Fellowship was Dewey Hickey. His wife, Harriet, was editor of the *Dakota Connection,* a Baptist paper for the Dakotas. I stayed in their home for the first month.

Tom and Lou Sherrill were to be out of town for three weeks and needed a house sitter. I moved into their home for the last month. Tom was director of missions for the western half of North Dakota. Lou was Woman's Missionary Union (WMU) director for the Dakotas. The two of them were God's special servants. They became very dear to me.

Another couple I met was Oscar and Helen Mason. Oscar was the volunteer coordinator for North and South Dakota. I had slides and projector with me; and as soon as Oscar found out, he began scheduling slide presentations all over the Dakotas. Helen was his associate in the fellowship office.

As they took me to the different churches for the slide presentations, they always made sure I got to see God's beautiful northern world. I enjoyed seeing Mount Rushmore in South Dakota and the Peace Gardens in Manitoba, Canada.

I was amazed at how far apart people lived. No wonder there are not very many churches. We did see volunteer teams building churches. It was a delight to learn all about their work. While I was in Bismarck, North Dakota, my church involvement was at Capitol Heights Baptist Church. I was able to do some bookkeeping, bank reconciliations, and financial statements for them while I was there.

I returned home in September 1989. I thought surely at the age of 69 I could settle down. After the foreign missions emphasis was over, I began to think about retiring. I was forced to look at my own financial situation and take an accounting of my own budget. During the spring of 1990, I concluded that my expenses were exceeding my income. I had two options—either change my lifestyle or find another source of income.

A good friend with whom I had worked in 1977 through 1979 called and asked if I would like to work for him part-time. In May 1990 I went to work for Frank Finch at Splice Co., Inc., located right here in Pell City. I worked for Frank until spring 1993, when I retired. The part-time work enabled me to have central heat and air installed in my little house and to buy a more reliable car. God in His infinite mercy had provided the answer to my needs every step of the way. He had promised that He would. He was faithful to His promises.

22

God's Precious Promises

"Delight thyself also in the Lord; and he shall give thee the desires of thine heart. Commit thy way unto the Lord; trust also in him; and he shall bring it to pass" (Psalm 37:4–5).

When God first called me to missions as a teenager, I dreamed of going to the Orient. In 1930 Kyle M. Yates served as interim pastor at First Baptist Church, Birmingham, Alabama. He always preached on missions. I can still hear him stating that China was requesting 900 missionaries. This was before the Iron Curtain was drawn. Many times I wondered if that curtain would have been drawn if we had sent those 900 missionaries into China. The longing to go to China never left me. I dreamed of going to China to share the gospel. As each assignment came I asked, *Heavenly Father, are You going to let me go to the Orient this time?* But I was always sent in another direction.

When Jolene Ivey called on March 21, 1990, to ask if I would like to go with a group of Woman's Missionary Union (WMU) women to an evangelistic crusade being held in Korea, my answer was "Yes! But I cannot afford the cost." She asked me to pray about it. If it was God's will, He would provide. This was my dream; but because I had bought my little house, I knew I could not afford to go to the Orient. Jolene said that if I really wanted to go, I should come to the state WMU convention in Montgomery that week. The group was to be commissioned at the convention on Saturday, March 24.

My immediate response was to call my pastor. I called his office but he was not in. His secretary, Nan Willis, said she would find him and have him call me. I walked to my front door, and guess who drove into my driveway? God is so good! I shared with him all that had happened. He asked, "Do you really want to go?"

I answered, "Yes! Do you know anyone who wants to buy a house?"

He advised me to go ahead and get ready. Everyone would pray about it. I told him I only had three days to decide.

He said, "Go ahead and be commissioned and we will see what we can do."

His faith has buoyed me every step of the way for the past ten years. No one was more supportive or encouraging than A. L. Courtney. I am positive God placed him in Pell City especially for me. I praise God for this!

I went to Montgomery and was commissioned with the other five women. God only asks that we take one step at a time. If we can see our way, fine, but if we cannot, we must walk by faith. Churches all over Alabama where I had shared my experiences learned of the coming trip to Korea. Many individuals and churches from all over the state contributed to the raising of the $5,000 needed for my trip. When the down payment was due, it was available. When the balance was due, it was available.

One particular gift came to the church from a lovely young woman. It had a note attached that read, "I have been wanting to do something special in memory of my husband, and knew immediately that this was what Bob would have wanted. Add this to Eunice's trip." Signed, Donna Rutherford. God did not answer in advance, but every day every need was supplied. He is so great!

Jerry Bedsole once told me to claim Psalm 37:4; "Delight thyself in the Lord, and he shall give thee the desires of thine heart." I did just that. I talked to the Lord about the Orient, placed it in His hands, and left it there. Even knowing that God does answer our prayers, I still could not comprehend that He was giving me this trip to the Orient! I had never seen the word *give* in that verse. I had always thought that if it was His will for me to go, then He would *let* me go, but I never dreamed He would just give me this trip.

To everyone who contributed to this experience, I say in Korean, *"Com sa ham ne da"* ("Thank you") for the generous way you responded to this Korean missions trip. God honored your trust and really poured out His blessings. The trip was beyond all I could ever ask or even imagine. The time was too short, but God did let me see a very short glimpse of China.

There were six WMU women going to Korea from Alabama. I was amazed at how God worked it all together. It was a miracle from the beginning. Jolene Ivey, associate to the executive director of Alabama WMU, and Elaine Stephens, from Foley, Alabama, were paired to be roommates and prayer partners. Methal Riggs, from Mount Hope, Alabama, was so excited at orientation, but the week before we were to leave she underwent open heart surgery and could not go. Carolyn Johnson from Birmingham, Alabama, had planned a trip to China the previous year, but because of political unrest in that country, the trip had been canceled. Her passport was current and she was delighted to take Methel's place. Carolyn was paired with Jean Broad from Huntsville, Alabama. My partner was Jo Langford from Foley, Alabama. Only God could have worked out all the partners so well. I enjoyed every minute with Jo.

Our first week was spent traveling, receiving orientation, and finally arriving Thursday by train in Pusan, Korea. We were met by a crowd of people at the station, holding banners and singing loudly. Each banner had a name on it. They were welcoming the volunteers. I was so completely astonished I forgot to get a picture of them. A man loudly called out "Eunice Perryman," and I went forward to meet my pastor and youth director for the next few days. I was escorted by Pastor Cho and Minister Lee, along with all of their group, across the street to the Arirang Hotel. They said they would come back for me at 7:00 P.M. in time to attend revival services which were to begin that evening.

From the beginning, it was clear to Jo and me that God had planned for us to be together. When we arrived in Korea, we were divided into teams. Each team had a US pastor. Our pastor was Gene McHargue from Hickory, North Carolina. He would be preaching at the revival service. Jo and I were to fill in anywhere we were needed. We loved every minute of it.

Friday morning Pastor Cho and Minister Lee took us from our hotel to the Yaen San Baptist Church where we were to work. Several women had come to join us for visitation. Several youth also joined us because school was not in session. Pastor Cho and Gene McHargue would visit in homes and offices. Jo and the pastor's wife were to also visit in the homes. Minister Lee and I were to work with the students. Minister Lee was a very able translator for me. Jo had a few problems because the pastor's wife did not speak much English and could translate very little.

We had been told to prepare for anything. I was glad we were warned. I held three sessions with students and one with some women on Friday. I asked if all the women were believers and Minister Lee said, "Yes. Teach Bible—no tract." For a long time afterward, I could not remember what I taught that day, but after much soul-searching and thinking, John 15:1–14 came back to me—a lesson about bearing fruit for Jesus Christ. Amazing! Koreans could teach me so much about bearing fruit. I felt so humbled, but God had used even that.

Minister Lee was an excellent youth director. After three sessions with small groups, four accepted Christ. God used it all and brought glory to Himself!

It was a special experience when Minister Lee first prayed for me. I felt the fervor of prayer that the Koreans are known for. He prayed for about ten minutes and in every other sentence came the name "Eunice Perryman." He was really striving in prayer. Even though he prayed in Korean and I had no idea what he was saying, I did know that I wanted God to answer according to His will. I said amen to it all. When he ceased and said, "Amen," I opened my eyes. The class still had their eyes closed and their hands uplifted, as if uplifting someone to God; then slowly their hands came down and their eyes opened. They were wet with perspiration and I felt as if I had been completely wrung out. Never have I experienced being so thoroughly lifted up in prayer. *Thank You, God, for that experience!*

Later that afternoon Minister Lee and I had a chance to sit down and talk. He said he had been at that church for two years and had seen only 11 conversions. I had been here only one day and had seen four. I saw that he needed much encouragement. I assured him that it was his preparation and seeking the lost that had made it possible. I told him God had honored his efforts. I assured him that I was only being used by God as an instrument in His holy hands. Minister Lee was such a dear, committed person. My soul was blessed in working with him. We returned to our hotel at 5:00 P.M. and left again at 7:00 P.M. for revival services. After each evening service we would go into a small office with the ministers and their wives for refreshments. They served us lovely fruits and drinks. We did not return until 11:00 P.M. My feet were swollen when I fell into bed. After all, I was 70 years old!

Saturday morning we began all over. At one point Minister Lee wanted me to take a few hours and visit in the homes. We met three young people on our way out. Two of them explained that the third young girl wanted to know how to be saved! The other two had brought her to us. We went back inside and shared Jesus Christ with her. She prayed to receive Christ then reached for some tracts to take to her friends. Unbelievable! Oh, how we could learn from the Koreans!

Our first visitation was with a woman at a well—a watering hole, really. A pipe came up out of the concrete and the women used it for a washing place. There was a woman there with whom they wanted me to talk. She was a Buddhist and had such a sad expression on her face. She shook her head, "No," from the very beginning. We shared the tract anyway, but she did not want to pray. I let her know I loved her and that Jesus would give her peace and a happy expression on her face. We told her as we left that we would love to have her come to church that night. It was a sad experience, but a learning one. I am so glad that God does not hold us responsible for results. He just wants us to go and share the gospel.

Our next visit was in a home with a small shop in front of

it. The woman seated us then left us to have a time of prayer while she prepared a drink. The drink was cold. I thought perhaps it was potato soup, but found that it was made from soy beans. We enjoyed our visit with her very much.

We returned to the church where the youth were ready to leave and hand out tracts. We walked with them for several blocks, inviting people to the revival and giving tracts in doorways. We had three more students accept Christ that day. When I arrived back at my hotel that evening at 5:00 P.M., my feet were so swollen I could barely walk. I fell into bed and could not go back that night. I really hated to miss it. I had given my testimony on Friday night and Jo was to give hers that night. She would also sing. I had no choice but to stay in bed, so I prayed for those who would be going to the revival.

Sunday was our last day in Pusan and we wanted to give it our all. Yaen San Baptist Church has a membership of about 120. The adults meet in homes for Bible study. Jo met with the preschool and children's department and I met with the older children and youth. I taught a lesson to the whole group and then they went into their separate classes.

We were treated to our very first Korean meal in a real Korean home. We had eaten in restaurants all week so this was a special treat. We sat on the floor. Our hostess set about 30 different dishes of food on the table and we were told to eat only what we wanted. They gave us forks but we wanted to use our chopsticks. We had been practicing! I tried most of the dishes, including three kinds of *kimchi,* a Korean pickled vegetable served with every meal. One of these was good but the others did nothing for me. The Koreans were delighted when they saw us enjoying their foods. It was a delight. That afternoon our pastor and his wife and Minister Lee asked to show us around Pusan, the beach, and the port. It was beautiful!

They left us at our hotel until time for Sunday night's special service. We had gifts for the church and took them with us that night. Much to our surprise we learned Americans cannot outgive Koreans! Jo and I were given lovely Korean dresses. They said mine was the national Korean wedding dress. We could not wait to try them on. Mine was too small, but I promised that when I needed a wedding dress, I would have it altered! It was a great evening. We received many other gifts from the church. The pastor gave us a beautiful plaque of appreciation. We had been told that if a person brags on anything a Korean has, he will give it to them. At lunch that day I had admired a pair of gorgeous, cloisonné chopsticks, but was careful not to say anything for fear they would insist I take them. We gave the pastor and his wife a large afghan with the outline of the state of Alabama worked into it. They were very pleased. We had many small gifts for our translators, also souvenirs from Alabama. One man gave us each a peace pipe. We were given scarves, dolls, scrolls, etc. We cried through most of the service and would have loved to stay longer if we had not been expected in Seoul and Hong Kong. The offering that Sunday had been $138 and they gave 50 percent of it to missions. We were told Korea supports 20 missionaries in the surrounding countries. I was amazed. How they put the US to shame.

Monday, August 13, we boarded the train back to Seoul. It was a lovely trip across the country, and best of all, the train was air-conditioned. By afternoon we were checked into our hotel and settled in for the week.

On Tuesday morning we held a victory breakfast and invited all the national pastors to join us with their wives and interpreters. It was a wonderful time. All 55 volunteers wanted to share their experiences. Our final reports showed more than 700 people had accepted Christ, most from the revival services. At Yaen San Baptist Church we had seen 27 conversions. There were a total of 1,000 rededications. It was really a praise service to Him Who is worthy!

That evening we went to the Olympic Stadium for the opening services of the Baptist World Alliance (BWA). The BWA meets only every five years. This was the 16th meeting. We had to ride two subway trains, trudging up and down the steps leading to the subways, leaving us exhausted. Even so, it was a very special evening. We were seated in a special section.

There was a parade of all the national pastors and ministers to welcome us. Following this, a group of young girls came out to the middle of the arena, gathered armloads of gifts, and came up into our area, giving every foreigner a gift. My gift was a beautiful, cuddly stuffed toy. They are very caring, loving, and giving people. Keith Parks, then president of the FMB, brought a message titled "Global Evangelism Now!"

One of the US volunteers fell and hurt himself on that first night. He had had a hip replacement and all those subway stairs had been too much for him. His hip was dislocated when he fell, and after two days of torture, they finally got it back into the socket and sent him home. The president of the Korean National Convention sent a bus for us each night after that making it a much better trip.

The prayertime held at the BWA meetings was very impressive. Everyone was asked to join hands in groups of four. People in Korea often pray aloud. Soon we were all praying aloud. Many times I would be holding hands with a Japanese, African, and Indian and none of us knew what the other was saying. At a given time the praying would grow quieter and someone from the podium would close the prayer. It was such an indescribable time!

There was a delegation of 100 Russian men attending the meeting. It was the first time they had ever been allowed to come. The president of the BWA commented that we were all looking forward to the day we could hold the BWA meeting in Russia or even in North Korea. When the Russians entered the auditorium, the whole congregation stood and applauded. God is so great!

The most beautiful experience was seeing the baptism of more than 8,000 people. More than 1,600 people who could not stay the entire week were baptized on Monday. The churches had postponed their converts' baptisms until the BWA meeting in hopes of reaching their goal of 10,000. The baptism was held at the Hahn River. It was a gorgeous site where the Olympic competitions had been held. The river was approximately two blocks wide and bleachers were set up on either side. The bank was rocky at the water's edge. All those participating were dressed in white robes. The sun was very hot. Speeches were made for about an hour before the pastors went into the water with their groups. One small group would huddle and pray and then the pastor would baptize each one in his group. This was spread out along three or four blocks of the riverbank. I made pictures, but they could not begin to capture what was really happening. It is impossible to describe it.

We slowly made our way toward the buses and were able to get on one going to the International Hotel, where we could get a subway back to our hotel. When we finally arrived at our hotel, the bus had already left for that night's meeting. We were disappointed, but did not have the strength to go anyway. We were leaving on Sunday morning for Hong Kong so we used this time to pack.

Our first stop was in Tokyo, where we had a five-hour lay-over. This put us in Hong Kong about 9:00 P.M. Each time we went into another country we had to go through customs. We finally settled into our hotel in Hong Kong about midnight. Missionaries Bob and Barbara Bradley, originally from Alabama, were there to help us. They had made arrangements for us to go into China on Wednesday! This would be the culmination of my dream! Bob and Barbara were preparing to return home for a furlough. They were so gracious to us. They invited us for supper one evening and served fried chicken, mashed potatoes, gravy, pinto beans, slaw, corn bread, and coconut and chocolate pies, with plenty of iced tea! Everything tasted so good! We all pigged out. It had been almost three weeks since we enjoyed good American food.

Wednesday was a special day. We made our way into China on a high-speed ferry. After going through immigration and customs in Macao, we rented a large van so the eight of us could travel together. Our driver and navigator made ten.

We soon spotted a small village perched on a hill; and because we had our own vehicle and could stop wherever we wanted, we went to see this quaint little village. It was a village much like Lottie Moon must have lived in. We saw no sign of commercialism there. Some of the buildings had only partial walls standing. They were very ancient. As we looked up we saw a television antenna and electric wires! Some of the villagers stopped what they were doing to watch us. On closer inspection we found that inside those ancient walls families had fashioned makeshift walls to make rooms. It was a most unusual experience and we were pleased that Bob and Barbara could speak their language.

At lunch we found ourselves in a little town at the Penthouse Restaurant. It was a revolving restaurant located in a hotel, so during our meal we saw the whole city. Before we knew it, it was time to turn back. We changed our *yuan* back into Hong Kong currency, went back through customs and immigration, and boarded the ferry back to Hong Kong. Needless to say, my passport is almost worn out!

Barbara helped us finish our shopping on Thursday as we prepared to leave on Friday. Our greatest disappointment was not being able to see the missions work going on in Hong Kong. Our group just did not have time. Part of our group gathered for a devotional time on Friday. We had all finished packing and needed this quiet time. It was a good feeling to load all our baggage and packages and head for home.

When we arrived back in Seattle, Washington, we again went through customs. We all had to pay customs tax on all we had bought. It was the first time I had ever had to pay, but I did not mind paying $41.60 one bit. It was wonderful that God had finally let me get a glimpse of China! It was such a short time that I could empathize with Moses when he was only allowed a glimpse of the Promised Land. I shall forever praise God for letting me have that wonderful glimpse of China. He is so great!

Epilogue

"But we have this treasure in earthen vessels, that the excellency of the power may be of God, and not of us" (2 Cor. 4:7).

As of August 1993 God is not through with me yet. I thought that retirement meant settling down. I remember years ago pledging that when I retired I wanted a rocking chair in every room; so that when I got ready to rock, a chair would be close by. That was not what God had in mind for me. God has continued sending opportunities to serve my way. I have yet to say no, even though I am nearing 73 years of age.

When invitations came, my gracious employer, Frank Finch, always let me go, realizing they were my first priority. Summer 1993 was spent completing this book. I thank God for letting me have this time to put it all together.

Recently God used me to lead a man to surrender his heart to the Lord. At his age of 45 he asked me to teach him how to study his Bible! A person won to Christ here in Pell City is just as precious as those in Ethiopia, Tanzania, or anywhere else in God's beautiful world. I just praise God for each opportunity.

Each Friday night I have an adult Bible study in my home. We are learning how to live the godly life God wants us to live. I also serve as WMU director of my church. Yes, dear ones, there is so much more God has for us to do.

If we cannot go, we can be a witness right where we are. It is good, physically and mentally, to be busy and to be needed. May God bless you all!

Simply His,

Eunice Perryman